The
Prisoner
and
the Kings

OTHER WORKS BY WILLIAM SEARS

BOOKS
Release the Sun
God Loves Laughter
Thief in the Night
The Wine of Astonishment
The Flame (with Robert Quigley)
A Cry From the Heart
All Flags Flying
Prince of Peace
Run to Glory
Tokoloshe
In Grandfather's Barn
Reminiscences I
The Half-Inch Prophecy
Reminiscences II

PLAYS
The Black Harvest
Dad Cashes In
The Undoing of Albert O'Donnell
The Turning of the Worm

TELEPLAYS
Dilemma in Donegal (with Robert Quigley)
Kid Gloves
In the Park (with Paul Ritts)

The
Prisoner
and Kings
the

How One Man
Changed the Course of History

by
William Sears

Bahá'í
PUBLISHING
Wilmette, Illinois

Copyright © 2007 by the National Spiritual Assembly of the Bahá'ís of the United States. All rights reserved.

The first edition of *The Prisoner and the Kings* was issued in 1971 by General Publishing Company Limited, Toronto. The revised second edition was published in 2007 by Bahá'í Publishing, 415 Linden Avenue, Wilmette, Illinois 60091-2844.

Printed in the United States of America on acid-free paper ∞

10 09 08 07   4 3 2 1

ISBN 10: 1-931847-41-X
ISBN 13: 978-1-931847-41-4

Library of Congress Cataloging-in-Publication Data
Sears, William.
    The prisoner and the kings : how one man changed the course of history
    / by William Sears. — Rev. 2nd ed.
        p. cm.
    Includes bibliographical references (p.   ) and index.
    ISBN-13: 978-1-931847-41-4 (alk. paper)
    ISBN-10: 1-931847-41-X (alk. paper)
        1. Bahá'u'lláh, 1817–1892. 2. Prophecies. I. Title.

BP392.S35 2007
297.9'3092—dc22

2006051749

Cover and book design by Suni D. Hannan

Contents

Preface to the First Edition

I have no doubt that someday soon talented and trained historians will record everything associated with the unique story told in these pages. The present author is not a historian. He makes no pretense of having set down a detailed or definitive historical picture of this turbulent period.

Yet, so powerful was the impact of these events upon me when I first encountered them that I felt impelled to share as much as lay within my power, however inadequate the attempt. I have outlined only a few of the more arresting themes running through the whole remarkable drama.

Future historians will properly evaluate these events, and will undoubtedly recognize in this story some of the chief motivations for many of the revolutionary changes that have taken place in the world since the middle of the nineteenth century.

William Sears
"Cherokee Smoke"
Palm Springs, California
November 12, 1969

Preface to the Second Edition

The Prisoner and the Kings offers a compelling look at the collapse of kingdoms and empires by juxtaposing commonly known history against the lesser-known story of the life of Bahá'u'lláh and His addresses to those kings and rulers that warned of their undoing. Bahá'u'lláh, the Prophet-Founder of the Bahá'í Faith, was a prisoner of the Ottoman Empire for most of His life. His bold pronouncements to the leaders of some of the world's mightiest nations might be surprising considering his status as a prisoner, but there is no doubt that the fates of these rulers followed the course that Bahá'u'lláh predicted for them.

The author, William Sears, was renowned during his life as a storyteller, and this book is written in his distinct, informal style. He did not intend it as a scholarly investigation of history, but rather as a brief and exciting glimpse into the dramatic parallels between the fate of monarchs and that of one whose life and teachings would come to change the world.

As Mr. Sears explained, future "trained historians" will shed more light on the events related in this book, but it was his excitement and enthusiasm for this epic story that compelled him. In composing this narrative, he drew on a variety of historical sources, including primary texts and Bahá'u'lláh's own writings. Endnotes are included for many of the references, though in some cases Mr. Sears included quotations ascribed to individuals that are meant to represent an impression of their thoughts and sayings, but are not direct quotes.

Thirty-five years after its initial publication in 1971, the story of *The Prisoner and the Kings* remains engaging and relevant. In preparation for this new edition, the book has undergone some additional editing, and chapter 15 has been updated to reflect changes and growth in the Bahá'í community.

Of particular interest is the fact that many of the translations of Bahá'u'lláh's writings that are included in this book were available only as extracts at the time of the book's initial publication. However, the recently published compilation *The Summons of the Lord of Hosts* contains not only full translations of Bahá'u'lláh's direct addresses to rulers such as Napoleon III and Pope Pius IX, but also the Súriy-i-Mulúk (Tablet to the Kings), which deals with Bahá'u'lláh's teachings on the necessities of kingship and the requirements of just rule. *The Prisoner and the Kings* serves as a complement to those original texts, and certainly anyone interested in the history that this book recounts will want to look to those writings, in addition to the available historical accounts.

A short note on the system of transliteration of Persian and Arabic names is also due, since the system used in this book differs from some others in its use of accents ("á" and "í") instead of overline ("ā" and "ī"), along with a few other differences. The names of individuals and some locations were transliterated following this style, for example "Ṭihrán" and "Náṣiri'iri'd-Dín Sháh" are used in place of the perhaps more familiar "Tehran" and "Nasiruddin Shah."

Mr. Sears's widow, Marguerite Reimer Sears, oversaw the preparation of this new edition, but sadly passed away shortly before work completed. She wished to express her gratitude to those who assisted her: Enayat Rohani for arranging the scan of the original book so it could be revised; Bill Barnes and Shirley Macias, who offered additional editing and revision; and Lorana Kerfoot, who proofread the revised book before it was passed to Bahá'í Publishing for publication.

PROLOGUE

The Prisoner and the Kings tells the story of the greatest mystery of modern times. Between 1867 and 1873 a solitary prisoner in a Turkish penal colony wrote a series of letters to the kings and emperors of the day that predicted with amazing accuracy the course of modern history: the fall of nations, the overthrow of individual monarchs, the decline of religious institutions, the rise of world communism, the birth of the State of Israel, and the threat of nuclear contamination.

The Prisoner was Bahá'u'lláh, one of the most remarkable figures in this or any age. What was the secret behind this handful of amazing communications? What was the source of the Prisoner's knowledge? And what did the letters have to say about us and our future?

The
Prisoner
and Kings
the

1 ❧ THE ASSASSINS

The Assassins

The uniform of Kaiser William I was splendor itself. His shining helmet glistened like a second sun as the royal carriage rolled majestically along the tree-lined avenues of Berlin.

The king smiled to himself. Where was there another monarch to rival him? He had humiliated France beyond his wildest dreams of vengeance. He had become the first Prussian king to rule the united German states as emperor.

Yes, there was reason to be pleased.

Suddenly the tranquil scene was shattered by the blast of a gun! A bullet plunged into the metal headgear of the kaiser, who slumped back onto the seat of his carriage, dangerously wounded. Panic ran through the streets of Berlin.

"Assassin! Assassin!"

William I would recover. The shot that had nearly ended his life, however, marked the opening of a series of disasters that struck his fellow monarchs in both Europe and the Orient. Most of the latter were not so fortunate as William.

Far away in Constantinople, a second king sat proudly on his throne. He, too, was both pleased with himself and totally unaware of a strange web of death that was gathering about the kings of the earth.

Sulṭán 'Abdu'l-'Azíz, ruler of the vast Ottoman Empire, had surrounded himself with a protective network of spies. They reported everything that might arouse the slightest suspicion of opposition to the crown. The sultan's enemies, however, were equally thorough.

Suddenly and without warning, the palace corridors were alive with hurrying feet: "Revolution!"

Color drained from the king's face. 'Abdu'l-'Azíz's cries for help echoed, unanswered, along the corridors. There was no place to hide.

The leaders of the revolt laid violent hands on him and imprisoned him within his own palace. There the fate that was pursuing the kings of the world overtook him. Early one morning, the "slayer" appeared.

With a thrill of horror word ran through the streets of Constantinople: "Assassin!"

A third king was marked for the same fate.

Alexander II Nicolaevitch, czar of Russia, was *not* pleased with himself. He lived in daily fear for his life. Guards patrolled outside his door. Even they were suspect, and were changed constantly. Every dish of food was tasted first by servants. The imperial bedchamber was searched each night before the czar would retire.

Stories of the king's obsession with fear circulated among his subjects. Alexander tried to disprove such damaging rumors by riding openly through the streets. In his heart, though, he dreaded these journeys and was constantly on the alert, watching for the unseen enemy.

The inevitable day came. There was a threatening movement in the crowd, and suddenly a bomb exploded in the path of the royal carriage. Guards seized the suspected assassin, and Alexander dismounted from his carriage to interview the prisoner. Before he could protect himself, the assassin's accomplice threw a second bomb, which exploded at the czar's feet. The crowd, appalled, fled in panic. Mortally wounded, Alexander II was carried back to his palace.

Before the afternoon was out, the whisper ran from one end of St. Petersburg to the other: "Assassin!"

A fourth king, on another continent, was caught up in the same whirlwind. Násiri'd-Dín Sháh, king of Persia, went blissfully on his way to offer prayers on the eve of his great Jubilee Festival. The shah* had carefully planned each step of this great celebration. It was to glorify his name and would be his eternal monument in history.

Suddenly, without warning, while the king was at prayers, a pistol shot echoed through the sacred shrine where the king prayed. Násiri'd-Dín Sháh fell to the floor. The chanting hushed. The royal tragedy of Berlin, St. Petersburg, and Constantinople had been reenacted in Ṭihrán. Another king lay dead.

Cries of panic rang out among the royal party. Courtiers ran to and fro, not knowing what to do. The prime minister, who had accompanied the shah, was devastated by the unexpected turn of events.

"The news must be concealed, at least until after the Festival," he ordered. "No one must know!"

The shah's body was carried secretly back to his carriage. The grand vizir climbed in behind the king, supporting the dead weight. He held the shah's body erect. Frozen in the silence of death, indifferent to the revelry around him, the king of all the Persians was driven back to his palace on the eve of his great Jubilee.

---

* Persian term for king.

Bonfires lighted the night skies. Banners waved everywhere. Trumpets flourished, cymbals crashed, the crowd cheered; all proclaimed the might and majesty of Náṣiri'd-Dín Sháh, who had described himself as the "king of kings." Gay festive band music blared out noisily as the carriage rolled on noiseless wheels through the streets.

Once within the palace gates, the shah's terror-stricken ministers passed along the dread words: "Assassin! Assassin!"

———— ❦ ————

2 ❧ THE PRISONER

Summon . . . the nations unto God.

The Prisoner

What fate bound together the tragic kings of Germany, Russia, Turkey, and Persia? Why had violence struck them down in almost the same hour?

Their story is one of the great dramas of our generation. Why haven't we heard more about it? These were not mythical kings. Their overthrow and destruction was not part of a historical novel. It was not a suspense story taken from the pages of popular fiction.

These were ruling monachs. They, and later their thrones, were swept away in a titanic upheaval that engulfed and swamped no less than twenty kingdoms in half a century. Indeed, the fate that overtook them has since seemed to pursue their elected successors in the republics that took the place of their fallen thrones.

The link binding together the four kings and their associates was a Prisoner, a solitary condemned figure in a cell in a Turkish fortress on the coast of Palestine. It would have been hard to find a candidate less likely to challenge the rulers of the world, or anyone more helpless, than the Prisoner Who arose to challenge them all.

Two of these same kings had already brutally persecuted and humiliated Him. Although determined to silence Him, they had been totally unsuccessful. Attempts to kill Him developed into almost a comedy of errors. Every stroke the kings devised to eliminate the Prisoner seems, in retrospect, to have raised Him and lowered themselves. Gradually, it was they who became prisoners and He who became, as one British historian has said, "The object of a love that kings might envy and emperors sigh for in vain."[1]

There has never been a story like it. The Prisoner was stoned three times. He was scourged until His skin was broken and the blood flowed from His body. He was weighted down with chains; a one-hundred-pound iron yoke lacerated His shoulders and scarred Him for life. His feet were locked in stocks. He was chained to His companions and to the floor of His prison. He was poisoned three times. The edicts of kings stripped Him of His wealth and position. He was torn away from his relatives and friends and banished from His native land forever. On four separate occasions He was exiled, each exile more cruel than the previous one. At last the kings banished the Prisoner to the most dreaded penal colony in the Near East, a place in which they felt certain He would perish. The final imprisonment locked Him up in a fortress surrounded by moats and battlements. He was encircled by enemies in an inhospitable climate, an area rampant with disease.

The kings were confident that the Prisoner would die and be heard of no more. That should have been the end of the story.

In fact, it was only the beginning. In the midst of death and suffering, the Prisoner foretold the coming collapse of the dynasties of each one of these kings. He described the inevitable extinction of their empires. His prophecies had a precision that was frightening. One solitary condemned exile, writing from prison in the historic "Holy Land," warned the kings of coming doom. One mysterious figure reached out His hand into both Europe and Asia and "shook the kingdoms" until the structure trembled and fell.

Yet, in spite of all that He had suffered at the hands of these rulers, the Prisoner offered to help them prevent the coming calamity. Had the rulers heeded His words, they could have avoided their fate. Instead, a flock of monarchs has vanished, one by one, from the contemporary scene.

Who was the Prisoner? And what did a condemned exile have to do with four of the mightiest monarchs of his day? The Prisoner declared that He had *everything* to do with both kings and governments. He told them plainly that His mission in life was to awaken the rulers of the earth to their social and spiritual responsibilities in a new age. The Prisoner said He was an instrument sent to protect the rights of the downtrodden and underprivileged. He challenged the kings in these words: "If ye stay not the hand of the oppressor, if ye fail to safeguard the rights of the downtrodden, what right have ye then to vaunt yourselves among men?"[2]

The Prisoner called upon the kings and leaders of men to unite in an energetic, worldwide effort so that the peoples of the earth might attain social justice and peace: "Arise thou amongst men in the name of this all-compelling Cause, and summon, then, the nations unto God."[3]

Why should any king pay attention to such ravings? Who would believe a madman who announced publicly the collapse of the world's greatest kingdoms? If He couldn't even save Himself from prison, how would He be able to control the destinies of kings?

Yet that is precisely what He did.

Kings were shut up in prison and the Prisoner was released. Monarchies were overthrown and vanished while the Prisoner's ideals have permeated the thinking of all humankind. It happened exactly as foretold in the letters from the prison cell in Palestine, and it happened with frightening precision, step-by-step, until each despot was dethroned, each king was shorn of his power, and the dynasty of each monarch was forever extinguished!

It is one of the most remarkable stories of our times.

———— ☙ ————

Give me a chance to
fling my stone in His face!

The Drama of the Báb

The story begins in Persia, in 1844. Despite the country's long history of cultural achievement, Persia in the nineteenth century was a land of almost unequaled corruption and decadence. The shah was a despot, his government conducted by an equal mixture of graft, flattery, and brutality. Day-to-day control of affairs was in the hands of venal politicians and fanatical clergymen.

Suddenly, at this lowest ebb in the country's history, a spiritual revolution broke out. No other nation in modern history has experienced anything like the nine years that followed. A radiant young man called the Báb (Arabic for "door" or "gate") arose to declare that the "Day of God" had dawned.

All over Persia, tens of thousands of people flocked to the new cause. The most ardent of them were students from the colleges and seminaries. For a moment in history, it looked as though the entire nation would accept the Báb's teachings of social justice and spiritual regeneration.

The clergy and the courtiers prevented this from happening. Realizing that their own privileges were endangered, they persuaded the shah that the Báb was a threat to the state. Although the Báb had shown every respect for civil authority, the shah chose the side of his advisers and launched a campaign of terror. Thousands of the Báb's followers were hounded throughout the country, betrayed, tortured, and massacred. Finally, on July 9, 1850, the Báb was executed.

One of the Báb's leading supporters was a young nobleman Who took the title "Bahá'u'lláh" (Arabic for "glory of God"). Because of the prominence of His family and the respect that His own life had won Him at the Persian court, Bahá'u'lláh was not killed in the general massacres. His leadership of the persecuted "Bábís" (as the Báb's followers were called), however, made Him a marked man.

Highly placed opponents of the Báb appeared determined to put Bahá'u'lláh to death. He was widely admired, however, and there was no believable pretext on which so prominent a personality could be condemned.

The needed pretext came in 1853, when two ignorant youths fired a shot at the king as he emerged on horseback from his palace. Immediately the responsibility was placed on all the followers of the Báb and Bahá'u'lláh. Implacable hostility swept the nation. All attempts to inquire into what had really happened were cast aside.

The shah, his ministers, the clergy, and the people united in relentless hate, delighted to have at last an excuse for annihilating the One Whom they had come to fear as a danger to the state.

Many who were merely thought to be friendly or sympathetic to the new faith were arrested and slain, unless they were wealthy and could fill the coffers of their persecutors. In Bahá'u'lláh's case, the authorities knew that the sentence of death and His execution must be done with cunning. Bahá'u'lláh and His family were still highly respected in the land. His father had been a highly esteemed and honored minister of state.

During those hectic days when one of the waves of persecution reached its peak, Bahá'u'lláh was a guest of the new prime minister, Mírzá Áqá Khán. He should have been safe there. This same prime minister was understood to have promised the Báb that he would protect the innocent victims of the king's wrath if the Báb would help the minister. The Báb had done so. Now Mírzá Áqá Khán faced the crisis of having to redeem that pledge.

No one knew better than the prime minister that Bahá'u'lláh was innocent of any crime. Unhappily for the soul of this troubled minister, his loyalties constantly fluctuated back and forth throughout his career. One moment he would be inspired to try and help the mistreated followers of the Báb, the next he would cringe in fear, dreading the loss of his position. He would then begin attacking them. In the end, fear pushed out courage and decency. It also precipitated the downfall and disgrace of the prime minister.

At first, Mírzá Áqá Khán tried to effect a reconciliation between the shah and Bahá'u'lláh. He sent a warm letter to

Bahá'u'lláh in Karbilá, Iraq—where Bahá'u'lláh had been exiled briefly by the previous prime minister—telling Him of these plans and inviting Bahá'u'lláh to return to the capital. For a month Bahá'u'lláh was the honored guest of Mírzá Áqá Khán. During this time a great number of notables and dignitaries from Ṭihrán flocked to meet Bahá'u'lláh. So much attention and honor was paid to Him that it aroused the envy and fury of His enemies.

Bahá'u'lláh was a guest in the village of Afchih when news came of the attempt made on the life of the shah.

He condemned the act in the strongest terms, but He also refused to listen to the pleadings of the prime minister's brother, who urged Him to flee into hiding in the neighborhood. Instead, Bahá'u'lláh set out on foot for the shah's residence, the headquarters of the Imperial Army in Níyávarán, to prove His innocence. He refused even the offer of an armed escort.

When Bahá'u'lláh reached the village of Zarkandih He was met and conducted to the home of the acting secretary of the Russian minister, Prince Dolgorukov. The news of Bahá'u'lláh's arrival was conveyed at once to Náṣiri'd-Dín Sháh. The king was greatly amazed at Bahá'u'lláh's boldness in coming directly to his encampment.

Prince Dolgorukov proposed to Mírzá Áqá Khán that he protect Bahá'u'lláh in his own residence from the enemies who sought His destruction. The prime minister was afraid to extend any further consideration to Bahá'u'lláh for fear he might permanently lose his own position and prestige. Bahá'u'lláh was therefore delivered into the hands of a group of His enemies among the military.

They stripped Him of His headgear. Barefoot, bareheaded, and in chains, Bahá'u'lláh was marched the full distance from

Shimírán to Ṭihrán under the blazing sun. Several times along the way, His outer garments were torn from His body by the soldiers and the mob. He was struck by the officers accompanying Him, overwhelmed with abuse and ridicule, and pelted with stones and refuse.

As Bahá'u'lláh was approaching the capital, a fanatical old woman rushed from the crowd with a stone in her hand. Her whole frame shook with rage as she raised the stone, but the procession was moving too rapidly for her to keep pace. She tried to overtake them, shouting, "I entreat you! Give me a chance to fling my stone in his face!"

Bahá'u'lláh saw her hastening after Him. He halted the guard long enough to give the old lady her chance, saying: "Deny her not what she regards as a meritorious act in the sight of God."[4]

———— ✒ ————

He bringeth out those which are bound with chains.

The Black Pit

Bahá'u'lláh was thrown into a subterranean dungeon called the Síyáh-Chál, the "Black Pit." There He was to spend four months.

The dungeon was pitch black. Bahá'u'lláh was led along a gloomy dark corridor, then down three flights of stairs to the underground pit.

His body was bent so that He could be chained to the floor. His captors also chained Him to His companions, and His feet were placed in stocks.

Bahá'u'lláh's fellow prisoners numbered about 140. Among them were thieves, highwaymen, and assassins. There was no outlet from the pit other than the one door they had entered. It was alive with rats, and a hotbed of disease. Chill, damp, and fever-ridden, the dungeon stank abominably from the constantly accumulating filth.

For three days and three nights Bahá'u'lláh received no food or drink. Two chains, each weighing nearly one hundred pounds, which were famously used only for punishing the most notorious criminals, were in turn fastened around His neck. An iron yoke lacerated His flesh. Sleep was impossible for Him.

Shortly after Bahá'u'lláh entered the prison, it became evident that there was no basis for the suspicions against Him. Still, He was kept chained in that loathsome place. Each day, the jailer would open the door, sending a shaft of light to penetrate the gloom, and would call out the names of those who were to be executed that day in the public square. The misery and suffering that befell these innocent victims of the wrath of their sovereign can hardly be imagined.

It was in that pestilential prison that the mission of Bahá'u'lláh began. Just as the dove had descended upon Christ in the river Jordan, heralding the beginning of His ministry, so did that same Holy Spirit touch Bahá'u'lláh in that odious pit, into which He had been cast by the king of Persia.

Bahá'u'lláh wrote of that occasion, saying, "One night, in a dream, these exalted words were heard on every side: 'Verily, We shall render Thee victorious by Thyself and by Thy Pen. Grieve Thou not for that which hath befallen Thee, neither be Thou afraid, for Thou art in safety. Erelong will God raise up the treasures of the earth—men who will aid Thee through

Thyself and through Thy Name, wherewith God hath revived the hearts of such as have recognized Him."[5]

Long afterward, Bahá'u'lláh, in a letter to Náṣiri'd-Dín Sh̲áh, spoke of the days which He had spent in that dark prison. He recalled the twenty long years during which He had borne in patience further imprisonments and banishments.

In spite of all this, Bahá'u'lláh still addressed the shah with patience, forgiveness, and loving-kindness, saying, "O King, . . . Of a verity, God hath made thee His shadow amongst men, and the sign of His power unto all that dwell on earth. Judge thou between Us and them that have wronged Us without proof. . . . They that surround thee love thee for their own sakes, whereas this Youth loveth thee for thine own sake, and hath had no desire except to draw thee nigh unto the seat of grace, and to turn thee toward the right hand of justice. Thy Lord beareth witness unto that which I declare."[6]

Bahá'u'lláh's words warned Náṣiri'd-Dín Sh̲áh that if he did not withdraw his hand from injustice, all his pomp would vanish. His wealth would be turned into poverty, and his glory into abasement. Bahá'u'lláh made it plain that the Word of God could not be restrained by the walls of prisons, and that He would come forth from prison to claim His kingdom, which was in the hearts of men. There could only be sorrow and despair, Bahá'u'lláh said, for a king who would not be warned. He wrote: "No doubt is there whatever that these tribulations will be followed by the outpourings of a supreme mercy, and these dire adversities be succeeded by an overflowing prosperity. We fain would hope, however, that His Majesty the Sh̲áh will himself examine these matters, and bring hope to the hearts. That which We have submitted to thy

Majesty is indeed for thine highest good. And God, verily, is a sufficient witness unto Me."[7]

The shah's only interest, from the beginning, was that he should hear no more about Bahá'u'lláh. The shah's mother was far more inflamed with anger against Him. She branded Bahá'u'lláh as the would-be murderer of her son and was determined to put Him to death. One of the strangest features of the story is that she and all her fellow conspirators were unable to convince the shah to give the order for Bahá'u'lláh's death. They broke their spears against a seemingly invisible armor of the spirit surrounding Him.

By coming "out of prison" and through "exile," Bahá'u'lláh would fulfill promises from the scriptures of all religions, just as He had fulfilled them by being cast into prison. Bahá'u'lláh would be freed and would proclaim His mission to the kings of the world. His followers would publicize His fame in every corner of the planet, sharing His letters to the kings with the heads of state in all parts of the world.

In the light of these events, the words from the world's scriptures of the past become even more striking.

There is no description of these events in all of the Old Testament that is more fascinating than that in Job and the Psalms. They tell of Bahá'u'lláh's imprisonment in the "pit," His "sufferings," His "deliverance," and the worldwide proclamation of His Faith.

The book of Job, in one single chapter, describes a prisoner who will be cast into a "pit," who will have His feet placed "in stocks," who will undergo great suffering and "pain," who will be "innocent," who will be touched by the "breath of God" and "utter" a message of "knowledge" and "wisdom" for mankind, who will be "delivered from the dungeon," from the plots of His "enemy," whose newfound knowledge will come "in the night" in a "vision," and who will "speak" to man not "once" but "twice."

This incredible account is matched by a similar description of the prisoner in the Psalms. He will be delivered from a "horrible pit," in His mouth God will put "a new song," His coming will be mentioned "in the volume of the book," He will not "conceal" His message, but will proclaim it to "the great congregation" of the world.

Job also said, "I know that my redeemer liveth, and that he shall stand at the latter day upon the earth." Job promised that this great One would "break in pieces mighty men" and "lead princes away spoiled." This same Job prophesied that the "lightnings" of the Lord would come in the last days and say: "Here I am!"

On May 24, 1844, the day following the birth of the Bahá'í Faith, Samuel F. B. Morse sent his first formal telegraph message flashing from Washington to Baltimore: "What hath God wrought!" The press of that day spoke of it as the "lightnings of Job."

Explorers have found Mycenae, Troy, and Cuzco with far fewer clues to go on than we have been given in our search for the Promised One, Bahá'u'lláh. The gold to be found in the teachings of Bahá'u'lláh outvalues them all.

———— ✿ ————

I do not know Him.

Sounds in the Night

During His four months' imprisonment in the darkness of that dungeon-prison, Bahá'u'lláh constantly cheered the hearts of His companions. He encouraged them to remain confident. He assured them that nothing could prevent the future triumph of God's faith.

Bahá'u'lláh, recalling those hours in the Black Pit, wrote: "We were all huddled together in one cell, our feet in stocks, and around our necks fastened the most galling of chains. . . . No ray of light was allowed to penetrate that pestilential dungeon or to warm its icy coldness. We were placed in two rows, each facing the other. We* had taught them to repeat certain verses which, every night, they chanted with extreme fervor."[8]

Bahá'u'lláh taught His fellow prisoners to chant the praises of God.

One row would chant, "God is sufficient unto me: He, verily, is the All-Sufficing!"

The second row would reply, "In Him let the trusting trust!"

The sound of their voices pealed out in the early hours of dawn. The echo of their singing was so loud that it resounded up from the depths of that dungeon and rang out across the square to the royal residence.

The sound awakened Náṣiri'd-Dín Sháh. It alarmed him. He could not determine what the noise was, nor from where it came. The shah sent a courtier and inquired:

---

* Bahá'u'lláh refers to Himself here with the royal "we."

"What is the meaning of this sound in the night?"

Náṣiri'd-Dín Sháh was told that it was the chanting of Bahá'u'lláh and His companions in the Black Pit prison.

"In spite of their sufferings," the shah was informed, "these mad ones sing the praises of God."

The king turned away in silence. He could not understand such enthusiasm in the face of the horrors and the threat of death with which he knew they were surrounded. He felt uneasy.

It would have unsettled him entirely had the shah been able to read the future. On the very site where he now listened to the God-intoxicated voices of Bahá'u'lláh's companions, a pen would soon set down the signature that would wipe away forever the dynasty of Náṣiri'd-Dín Sháh and all the Qájár kings.

Kings of Persia would live to see the shattering fulfillment of the prophecies pronounced against them by Bahá'u'lláh, Whom they had condemned to imprisonment and exile.

In spite of the plots to destroy Him, no evidence whatsoever could be found implicating Bahá'u'lláh in the crime of which He was accused.

This forced His enemies to devise fresh schemes in order to assure Bahá'u'lláh's death. They sent for a young man named 'Abbás. He had been assisting them by pointing out the followers of the Báb on the streets of Ṭihrán, and they decided to use him to implicate Bahá'u'lláh in the attempt on the shah's life.

'Abbás had met Bahá'u'lláh many times in the past. The authorities promised 'Abbás a generous share of the money that they would be able to confiscate from Bahá'u'lláh's possessions, if only 'Abbás would point to Bahá'u'lláh and say, "Yes, he too is guilty."

"We need only one such witness," they told him.

The mother of the shah was particularly insistent. "What a humiliation for me!" she deplored. "That the mother of the shah should not be able to inflict on a prisoner the punishment which he deserves."

The old queen promised 'Abbás a rich reward if he would betray Bahá'u'lláh into her hands. She ordered the young man to go into the pit and look into Bahá'u'lláh's face. She told him that he would see in that face the would-be murderer of her son.

'Abbás was led into the presence of Bahá'u'lláh, not once, but several times. Each time the young man met Bahá'u'lláh, he stood transfixed, gazing upon the Prisoner's face, but then said, "I do not know Him."

And then he would turn away and leave.

No threat or promise of riches could persuade him.

Pain and suffering
were written on His face.

The Weight of Chains

Bahá'u'lláh's enemies failed in all their attempts to destroy Him. Yet the publicity that the charges had received among both the public and foreign embassies required some action. When they realized they would be unable to execute Him publicly, they resorted to cunning, deciding upon poison.

A few of those in authority, hoping to curry favor with the shah's mother and perhaps receive a generous and grateful gift of money, hatched a plot to kill Bahá'u'lláh secretly before He was released from prison. They intercepted the food that was being sent to Bahá'u'lláh and mixed it with what they felt would be a fatal dose of poison.

Even this attempt failed.

Bahá'u'lláh became desperately ill, and His agonies in that dungeon were greatly increased. He suffered from severe ill-health for years because of this poisoning attempt, but to the frustration of His enemies He did not succumb to it.

Bahá'u'lláh's eight-year-old son, 'Abdu'l-Bahá, visited His father while Bahá'u'lláh was a prisoner in the Síyáh-Chál. 'Abdu'l-Bahá's account of that meeting tells how terribly altered Bahá'u'lláh appeared. Pain and suffering were written on His face.

'Abdu'l-Bahá recalled that sad and moving scene: "His hair and beard [were] unkempt, His neck galled and swollen from the pressure of a heavy steel collar, His body bent by the weight of His chains." The sight made a never-to-be-forgotten impression on the mind of a sensitive boy.[9]

This was but the beginning of nearly half a century of such persecution and suffering.

What seems incredible about the story to us today is that at no time did Bahá'u'lláh's persecutors lay any formal charges against Him. At no time was He given the opportunity of a proper trial. None of the sufferings inflicted on Him resulted from a conviction for any crime. A lifetime of banishment, abuse, and imprisonment was inflicted on Him solely on the personal authority of two royal dictators.

The demand that Bahá'u'lláh's story makes on us goes far beyond one of mere human sympathy. The life of the Manifestation of God is as prophetic as His teachings are. In Jesus's sufferings were prefigured those of the peoples of the Mediterranean world who had rejected His message of peace and brotherhood.

Were millions of men in the twentieth century to follow Bahá'u'lláh down the path of exile, humiliation, imprisonment, and suffering to which the leaders of men had condemned Him?

The answer lay with the rulers who held the real power in the world of the nineteenth century—the kings and leaders of the great nations of Europe: France, Britain, Russia, and Germany.

To these men the Prisoner addressed Himself.

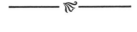

3 ❧ THE FIRST KINGDOM FALLS

Not liberty, equality, and fraternity,
but cavalry, infantry, and artillery.

The Mighty Bell

"O King of Paris! Tell the priest to ring the bells no longer. . . .
The Most Mighty Bell hath appeared."[1] These were the opening words of a letter that Bahá'u'lláh addressed to Napoleon
III, the emperor of France and nephew of Napoleon I. The
Prisoner told the emperor that this "Mighty Bell" was Himself and that He had come so that the "world might be quick-
ened, and all its peoples united"![2]

A remarkable sequence of events brought Bahá'u'lláh from
the Black Pit of Ṭihrán to the Turkish fortress of 'Akká on the
coast of the Mediterranean, from which He wrote this letter.
Not the least remarkable feature of the story is the precision
with which these events had been foretold in the scriptures of
three world religions.

We will want to return to those events when we consider
the fate of Náṣiri'd-Dín Sháh and the Persian monarchy. The
shah was not, however, the first ruler to receive a specific summons from the Prisoner. That ruler was Napoleon III, the most
powerful monarch of his day. It may help, therefore, if we
jump ahead a few years in time to the story of this king's historic encounter with the Prisoner.

Bahá'u'lláh wrote not once but twice to Napoleon. It is reported that he cast the first letter aside angrily and ridiculed
its contents. Napoleon was the first Western ruler to whom

the Prisoner sent one of His history-making letters. He was also the first ruler to be caught up in the rushing winds about which the letters spoke.

In the very year when the Báb first announced the advent of the Prisoner, 1844, Louis Napoleon was inspired to write a treatise on the elimination of poverty. The king appeared to be in tune with the spirit of the teachings of the Prisoner. The abolition of extremes of poverty and wealth was one of the basic principles that the Prisoner urged the kings of the earth to bring about.

"March at the head of the ideas of your century," Napoleon III reportedly declared, "and these ideas follow and support you. March against them and they overthrow you."

In sixteen years the emperor led his nation into three wars that ruined France economically. Louis Napoleon was given the opportunity to become an instrument to advance the welfare of mankind but was unable to put aside his own desires. His fate intertwined with that of the Prisoner time and again.

In the year of Louis Napoleon's death, 1873, the Prisoner wrote His greatest book, the Kitáb-i-Aqdas,[3] which contained yet other appeals to the kings and rulers of the earth, including a special message to the presidents and rulers of the republics of the West. He also laid down the fundamentals for a peaceful and ordered society and described the institutions by which this goal could be accomplished. Napoleon III professed to be a leader dedicated to such aims for social justice.

Throughout his career Louis Napoleon was motivated, he said, by "a social, industrial, commercial, humanitarian idea." When Napoleon III turned away from those principles, his downfall began.

The Prisoner wrote from the fortress-city of 'Akká: "O King of Paris . . . We tested thee, and found thee wanting. . . . Hadst thou been sincere in thy words, thou wouldst not have cast behind thy back the Book of God. . . . We have proved thee through it, and found thee other than that which thou didst profess."[4]

There is no place here for a detailed study of the relationship between the Second Empire and the rise of the worldwide following of the Prisoner. This story can do no more than give a few brief kaleidoscopic glimpses into those events that should have shaken and awakened the world.

It is our great loss that the world remained asleep.

The scratchings of a Pen.

The Hidden Scroll

If anyone had suggested that Louis Napoleon's predecessor, the great Napoleon I, would be turned back from his first conquests by a "pimple," the fortress of 'Akká, he would have been considered unbalanced. Yet Napoleon I himself admitted that he had been beaten, not by the British or the Turks, but by a "grain of sand" known as 'Akká.

When, half a century later, a contemptible Prisoner of the Turks sent out a message from that same city predicting collapse of the entire Napoleonic dynasty, the world was equally unimpressed.

Bahá'u'lláh, it was said, enchanted those who came to visit Him in that prison-city. The Turkish officials at first found this amusing. Especially so when a respected French agent of Louis Napoleon's government became a devoted friend of this condemned Prisoner.

The influence that the Prisoner gradually began to exert over all those who came to see Him became so great, however, that the guards grew suspicious of every visitor. Each one was kept under careful scrutiny. None was allowed to carry messages either to or from the Prisoner.

In spite of this close surveillance, it was not possible to prevent the Prisoner's second historic letter to Napoleon III from leaving the prison-city.

The letter was carried by a visitor. Though the guards searched him thoroughly, still they found nothing concealed on his person. The visitor must have smiled to himself as he hurried away, confident that the guards would never think to search beneath his hat. He walked nonchalantly through the streets of 'Akká, carrying in that hiding place Bahá'u'lláh's letter.

The letter was delivered to the French agent in 'Akká, who made the necessary translation and arranged to put the letter into the hands of the emperor.

The fate of a king, a nation, an empire, and a dynasty were all foretold on that scroll of paper hidden beneath the headdress of a visitor to a condemned Prisoner in the fortress of 'Akká.

————— ❧ —————

Thine empire shall pass from thine hands,
as a punishment for that which thou hast wrought.

The Day of Reckoning

The court of Napoleon III was the talk of all Europe. It was no make-believe king whose dramatic fall the Prisoner had predicted.

The ceremony and pageantry of Napoleon's court had become the envy of his neighbors. His contemporaries were overwhelmed by his lavish display. His ship rode on the crest of the waves. He himself could hardly believe his own good fortune. It surpassed even his fondest dreams. Napoleon III would make of his kingdom what he wished. Every golden door was opening—the world was his!

The Prisoner addressed Napoleon, "It beseemeth the king of the age to inquire into the condition of such as have been wronged, and it behooveth him to extend his care to the weak."[5]

Napoleon III was interested in the strong, not the weak, in the rich, not the poor. Least of all was he interested in the denizens of Turkish prisons. He was in fact the ally of those same Turks against the czar of Russia. The Crimean War had been his chance to avenge his uncle, the great Napoleon I, and the emperor had no desire to incur the disfavor of his Turkish allies.

Louis Napoleon's actions said plainly: "Don't bother me with trifles! The world is at stake!"

It was Napoleon's own world that was at stake. And he had already lost it. Following the initial contempt shown by Louis

Napoleon, the Prisoner wrote in his second letter to the French emperor, "O King! . . . . Arise, and make amends for that which hath escaped thee. Ere long the world and all that thou possessest will perish, and the kingdom will remain unto God, thy Lord and the Lord of thy fathers of old. It behooveth thee not to conduct thine affairs according to the dictates of thy desires."[6]

The Prisoner warned the emperor that unless his misdeeds were immediately corrected he would pay a terrible penalty: "For what thou hast done, thy kingdom shall be thrown into confusion, and thine empire shall pass from thine hands as a punishment for that which thou hast wrought."[7]

The day of reckoning was on its way.

We see abasement hastening after thee.

The Swift Decline

It was the beginning of the end for the Napoleonic dynasty. Napoleon III had provoked the Crimean War in order to satisfy his inner anger against the Russian emperor. He had longed to rip up the treaty of 1815 and avenge his uncle's disaster at Moscow.

Another great inspiration of Napoleon III's reign had been to establish an empire in Mexico. He had conceived the grandiose idea before becoming emperor. Napoleon envisioned for himself a "new Constantinople" on the Isthmus of Panama.

He would be a monarch in both the East and the West and would establish his influence in the center of America.

Oddly enough, Bahá'u'lláh had promised Napoleon III almost that exact reward if the king would devote himself to the cause of unity and justice for all mankind. The Prisoner wrote, "O King of Paris! . . . Arise thou to serve God and help His Cause. He, verily, will assist thee with the hosts of the seen and unseen, and will set thee king over all that whereon the sun riseth."[8]

Napoleon III made no attempt to assist the Prisoner or listen to his words.

Napoleon III's American venture came to a dismal failure, and all of his subsequent attempts at expansion were overtaken by the same fate.

Suddenly, the old days of glory were gone. Earlier he had defeated both Russia and Austria in the Crimean and Italian wars. He had surpassed two of the most feared military powers in all Europe and had astonished the entire world. When Prussia and Austria went to war with one another in 1866, Napoleon III sat on the sidelines. He planned to intervene on the "proper" side at the "proper" time—that is, on whichever side would bestow upon him the greater benefit.

He guessed wrong and placed his fortunes with Austria, which Prussia overwhelmed swiftly and decisively. Napoleon's error was the first of a host that were to multiply and haunt him as his prestige declined.

It is written in the Bible that God punishes the kings and the nations. Louis Napoleon is almost a classic example of this principle at work. In reality, kings and nations punish themselves. They bring on their own sufferings by their wrong decisions.

In this Day of God, whenever a ruler acts unjustly in order to assure his own advancement or prestige, or that of his country or people, at the expense of others, the decisions made to achieve that ignoble end plant the seeds of disaster. The more opposed these decisions are to the fundamental Laws of God concerning justice, the greater will be the disasters and the more certain the downfall of all those who make such decisions. However long the process, the end is always the same.

The Prisoner tried to explain this basic principle to the leaders of the world. His mission was to call their attention to the Laws of God. If they disobeyed them, the resulting punishment would be brought on by their own wrong decisions. That is how God "punishes" the kings and the nations: they punish themselves.

Kaiser William I, ruler of Austria, later declared that this war of 1866, during which Napoleon III sat on the sidelines, was the ruin of France.

The kaiser remarked that Napoleon should have attacked from the rear.

It was too late. The "shining hour" had passed, and Napoleon III had no refuge now except in war. Already he was risking an imminent revolution at home. In July 1870, Napoleon III led his nation into war against Prussia.

The French minister of war proudly declared that France expected a great and total victory. History shows how pathetic this decision was—wrong decisions on all sides became the trademark of Napoleon III.

Chaos reigned unchecked: "Frequently soldiers and even generals went astray, not able to find their places. 'Have arrived at Belfort,' telegraphed General Michel on July 21st. 'Can't find my brigade; can't find the general of the division.

What shall I do? Don't know where my regiments are.' It has been observed that this document is probably unique in military records."[9]

The fulfillment of the promise made to Napoleon III by the Prisoner of the Holy Land had begun: "For what thou hast done, thy kingdom shall be thrown into confusion. . . ."[10]

In an attempt to prevent mutiny, Napoleon joined the army personally, along with his young son. Exhausted by the pressures on him, and with his health undermined by agonizing attacks of kidney stones, the emperor was barely able to stay on his horse during parade. It is said that he rouged his cheeks to disguise his pallor from the troops.

Napoleon III advanced with his army into oblivion.

The French agent in 'Akká became a follower of the Prisoner when he saw the devastating fruition of those very prophecies that he himself had translated into French and forwarded to Napoleon III.

They . . . made Us, with glaring injustice,
enter the Most Great Prison.

The Tide Turns

When we contrast the life and position of Bahá'u'lláh with that of Napoleon III at the beginning of the emperor's reign, then witness how their positions were completely reversed at the end, we begin to understand the true significance of the warning that the Prisoner sent to the king: "Hath thy pomp made thee proud? By My Life! It shall not endure; nay, it shall soon pass away, unless thou holdest fast by this firm Cord. We see abasement hastening after thee, while thou art of the heedless."[11]

Words that 'Abdu'l-Bahá used in another connection seem to apply with a special aptness to Napoleon III of France: "This glory shall be turned into the most abject abasement, and this pomp and might converted into the most complete subjugation."[12]

It would be difficult to imagine a contrast greater than that between Napoleon III and the Prisoner. In the year 1852, Louis Napoleon had been raised up to become emperor of France. In that same year, Bahá'u'lláh was arrested in far-off Persia and was marched for miles, bareheaded and barefoot in the blazing sun. He was led through a screaming mob of enemies. He was without food or drink during those hours when Napoleon III dined sumptuously in the capital of a brilliant empire.

In January 1853, Napoleon III married the Spanish Countess Eugenie de Montijo. The emperor's life was just becoming settled and his family established securely on the throne of France. In that same month, the Prisoner was uprooted from his home, robbed of His position and wealth, and banished forever from His native land.

The higher the tide of Napoleon III's power, the lower had seemed to ebb the fortunes of the Prisoner of the Holy Land.

Bahá'u'lláh was exiled like Abraham, stoned like Moses, scourged like Christ. He was imprisoned, chained, poisoned, and persecuted from city to city. At last He had arrived at that most dreaded of all Turkish prisons, the fortress of 'Akká, standing in the shadow of Mount Carmel, a Hebrew name meaning the "Vineyard of God." From that prison-city, He had sent His second letter to the emperor of France.

From that point on, with swift strokes from the hand of destiny, the Prisoner was raised up, and His teachings spread into every corner of the planet, while the emperor was toppled from the heights and his grandeur entirely eclipsed.

We shall never know what thoughts went through Louis Napoleon's mind as he was taken prisoner by a foreign king, following his defeat at the battle of Sedan. Did he recall those words once directed to him by the Prisoner of 'Akká? It is unlikely that Napoleon III grasped any part of the spiritual revolution that was already agitating the face of society. He was blind even to the part he, himself, was playing in this unfolding drama.

———— ❦ ————

God shall, assuredly,
judge with truth.

The First Kingdom Falls

The letters to Napoleon III from the prison-city of 'Akká contained several ominous prophecies.

The Prisoner prophesied that He would soon change fortunes and fates with all tyrant monarchs. Their positions in life, He said, would be reversed through the power of Almighty God. There was no king whose fate fitted those words better than Napoleon III of France: "Hearken, O King, to the speech of Him that speaketh the truth. . . . The tribulations that have touched Us, the destitution from which We suffer, the various troubles with which We are encompassed, shall all pass away, as shall pass away the pleasures in which they [the King's Ministers] delight and the affluence they enjoy."[13]

The Prisoner described the great reversal that would take place: "The days in which We have been compelled to dwell in the dust will soon be ended, as will the days in which they occupied the seats of honor. God shall, assuredly, judge with truth between Us and them, and He, verily, is the best of judges."[14]

Louis Napoleon lived to see these words come true.

The Prisoner had written: "O King . . . For what thou hast done, thy kingdom shall be thrown into confusion. . . . Commotions shall seize all the people in that land."[15]

Paris was besieged by the Germans. All resistance melted and the city capitulated. The French people were shocked by the cardboard collapse of their military might—they blamed the emperor. The Franco-Prussian War was followed by civil war, a period called the "terrible years" that exceeded in ferocity the war itself and left scars on the French mind, which affect France to this day. Confusion seized the entire nation, and suffering from famine, revolution, and disease took thousands of lives in Paris, Napoleon's "City of Light."

The Prisoner had told Napoleon: "We see abasement hastening after thee . . . a punishment for that which thou hast wrought."[16]

The emperor became the most thoroughly hated man in all of France. Mobs in Paris cried out for revenge against him and blamed him for the humiliation of France. Empress Eugenie barely escaped with her life, and the monarchy was extinguished.

Napoleon had one son, Prince Eugene Louis Jean Joseph, who had been educated in England. Even after his own fall, Napoleon III hoped for a future restoration of the Napoleonic throne with his son as emperor. Mercifully, he did not live to see the prince killed in the far-off Zulu war fought between the blacks and whites in South Africa.

The Prisoner's prophecies had indeed been "terrible" to one of "the kings of the earth" as the Bible had centuries earlier warned. The prophet Isaiah, in a single chapter, declared that a day would come when the kings would be punished. The Lord, Isaiah warned, would turn the earth "upside down" in that day, and He would "scatter" the inhabitants. The "haughty" and proud ones would "languish" away because of their wickedness.[17]

In order that there might be no mistake about whom Isaiah was speaking, the Prisoner Himself had written: "I am the One Whom the tongue of Isaiah hath extolled. . . . Blessed be the king whose sovereignty hath withheld him not from his Sovereign, and who hath turned unto God with his heart."[18]

Napoleon III had failed to meet the test of God and "went down to dust." He suffered the fate foretold for such kings by Isaiah so long, long ago: "And it shall come to pass in that day, that the Lord shall punish the host of the high ones that are on high, and the kings of the earth upon the earth."[19]

The first kingdom had fallen.

---

4 ✠ THE SECOND KINGDOM FALLS

He went down to dust in great loss.

The God of Battles

On June 18, 1871, Kaiser William I, emperor of Germany, entered Berlin at the head of his victorious troops. It was a day of great rejoicing. Napoleon III's armies had been crushed. William I was a national hero in Germany—he was becoming legendary. As the clattering hoofbeats of victory rang through the streets of Berlin, the emperor was the cynosure of all eyes.

He had achieved almost every dream. He had become, in turn, prince, king, and now emperor of a united Germany. There was no one to challenge him.

And then one voice was raised in warning. From His far-off prison cell, Bahá'u'lláh reminded the kaiser of what had befallen the emperor of France. He warned William that exactly the same fate awaited him if he did not follow the counsels that God was offering to the kings of the earth and devote himself to the service of unity and justice.

The Prisoner addressed these words to William I: "O King of Berlin! . . . remember the one whose power transcended thy power [Napoleon III], and whose station excelled thy station. Where is he? Whither are gone the things he possessed?"[1]

The victor, like the vanquished, was given the opportunity to respond to the call of God. Kings were trustees of God and were responsible for that trust.

The Prisoner warned Kaiser William I not to forget the lesson given to the world by the tragic fate of Napoleon III. "Think deeply, O King," Bahá'u'lláh wrote, "concerning him

47

[Napoleon III], and concerning them who, like unto thee, have conquered cities and ruled over men. The All-Merciful [God] brought them down from their palaces to their graves."[2]

The emperor, however, had always been convinced that Prussia was the rightful head of all Germany. He had always believed that only one thing would ever put her there: the force and power of a mighty army. History appeared to have proved him, not the Prisoner, to be right.

But the Prisoner was not only counseling the kings of the world, He was also warning them. Kaiser William I of Germany was no exception to the following warning of God: "O Oppressors on earth! Withdraw your hands from tyranny, for I have pledged Myself to never forgive any man's injustice."[3]

Up to the time of his accession to the throne, William had spent his entire time in the army. He has been described as militaristic and autocratic to the very extreme. He admitted that he believed only in the "God of battles."

The Prisoner warned the emperor: "O King of Berlin. . . . Take warning, and be not of them that are fast asleep. He [Napoleon III] it was who cast the Tablet [letter] of God behind him. . . . Wherefore, disgrace assailed him from all sides, and he went down to dust in great loss. Think deeply, O King. . . . Be warned, be of them who reflect."[4]

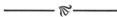

Be united, O kings of the earth, for thereby will the tempest of discord be stilled amongst you.

The Sound of War

William I did not listen to the warning from the Prisoner of 'Akká. His death delivered Germany into the hands of his reckless and arrogant grandson, the young William II. The new kaiser embarked on a cause that was directly opposed to almost every one of the Prisoner's counsels. Instead of bringing peace and tranquillity to his people and nation, he set in motion the forces of a military machine that was to engulf his nation in disaster. In the end, it was to shatter the peace of the world.

In 1898 Kaiser William II visited the Holy Land. The king was within a few miles of the prison-city where the Prisoner had addressed the historic message to his grandfather that foreshadowed the downfall of the Hohenzollern dynasty.

During that visit to the Holy Land, Kaiser William II allied himself with one of the Prisoner's most notorious persecutors, the sultan of Turkey. When he arrived in the Holy Land, one of the gates of Jerusalem was torn down and widened so that proper respect and honor could be paid to this visiting monarch.

Very different had been Bahá'u'lláh's arrival in the Holy Land. His party of exiles had been crowded into a small boat, delayed for hours, and then transported across the bay to the fortress-city of 'Akká. He was marched through the streets, humiliated by the mob, and finally cast into the fortress-prison.

Seventy-eight persons were crowded into one room with Him. They were all deprived of food and water. Most of them fell ill with malaria or typhus, and some died. All of this came by the edict of a sultan of Turkey, a throne on which William II now lavished his praise.

The kaiser on that occasion described himself as a friend of the caliph, 'Abdu'l-Hamíd of Turkey, and published the news of his affiliation with Turkey while in Jerusalem. He was proud of this new partnership of kings: kaiser and sultan would stand against the world.

But the kingdom of each of these friends was soon to collapse almost simultaneously, and their dynasties were to disappear forever in almost the same hour.

How aptly the Prisoner's words apply to William II during those days that the king spent in the holy city, Jerusalem. The kaiser made no effort to seek out the Prisoner or to inquire about Him. In fact, the kaiser ignored everything to do with the Prisoner and His teachings. If they had ever crossed the king's mind, no doubt he dismissed them as nonsense. The ravings of a religious fanatic had nothing to do with him, an absolute monarch. William dealt in more important things— like war. His fellow rulers would have agreed heartily; they had better things to do than visit prisoners.

Bahá'u'lláh's words challenged these assumptions: "O kings of Christendom! . . . Ye welcomed Him* not, neither did ye seek His Presence, that ye might hear the verses of God from His own mouth, and partake of the manifold wisdom of the Almighty. . . . Ye have, by reason of your failure, hindered the breath of God from being wafted over you, and have withheld from your souls the sweetness of its fragrance. . . . Ye, and all ye possess, shall pass away. . . . Ye shall . . . be called to account for your doings."[5]

---

* Jesus Christ

Powerful language. Very annoying to kings. Disturbing and upsetting to us as well, perhaps. Humanity as a whole has tended, as an initial reaction, to automatically reject anyone who claims to speak in the name of God. Yet our civilization, particularly its moral values, arose from the teachings of God. This was the authority with which Moses and Christ had spoken in the past.

———— ❧ ————

The rights and privileges of
all men must be protected.

The Unsheathed Sword

The solution to the problems of the world as expressed by the Prisoner and by William II could not have been more directly opposed.

The Prisoner wrote, "O kings of the earth! . . . Compose your differences, and reduce your armaments, that the burden of your expenditures may be lightened, and that your minds and hearts may be tranquilized."[6]

William II, on the other hand, agitated differences among his neighbors. He increased his armaments. He laid each day a heavier burden upon his peoples, unsettling a civilized nation with dreams of war and bloodshed.

The Prisoner declared, "O kings of the earth! . . . Heal the dissensions that divide you, and ye will no longer be in need of any armaments except what the protection of your cities and territories demandeth."[7]

William II established war as the religion of his country. He loathed any suggestions concerning disarmament or peace. He scoffed at the conclusions arrived at by the Hague Peace Conference in 1898. Commenting on one of them, the kaiser frankly that admitted he despised all such peace conferences. He showed his contempt in these words: "I trust in God and in my unsheathed sword, and I—on all resolutions of international conferences."

The advice of the Prisoner was exactly opposite to such an attitude. He said the "peace and tranquillity of the world" depended upon the leaders of mankind coming together in a "vast assemblage." They must consult in a spirit of good will upon this all-important matter, peace.

The Prisoner wrote, "Such a peace demandeth that the Great Powers should resolve, for the sake of the tranquillity of the peoples of the earth, to be fully reconciled among themselves. . . . We fain would hope that the kings and rulers of the earth, the mirrors of the gracious and almighty name of God, may attain unto this station, and shield mankind from the onslaught of tyranny."[8]

A clash between the vision of the Prisoner and that of the Hohenzollern kings was inevitable.

We desire that the differences of race be annulled.

The king of kings and the "King of Kings"

Kaiser William II lay with considerable elegance and diplomacy during the early days of his reign. He was particularly fond of invoking divine approval, and called upon Christ Himself when he assumed the kingship. Summoned to the throne of his fathers, it was with eyes raised to the King of Kings that he claimed to assume the scepter.

Like his grandfather before him, William II ignored all advice. He scorned all warnings. He knew where his duty lay. He didn't need the counsel of others to tell him that Germany must be supreme.

The Prisoner had advised the rulers of men otherwise: "O kings . . . God hath committed into your hands the reins of the government of the people, that ye may rule with justice over them, safeguard the rights of the downtrodden, and punish the wrongdoers. If ye neglect the duty prescribed unto you by God in His Book, your names shall be numbered with those of the unjust in His sight. Grievous, indeed, will be your error."[9]

But Kaiser William II was unmoved by wise counsel and words of caution, from whatever source they might come. "I regard myself as an instrument of heaven," Kaiser William told his people. "I go my way without regard to the events or opinions of the day."

He possessed a rage for personal power so great that he could no longer tolerate the annoyance of sharing decisions, even with his famous chancellor Otto von Bismarck. In March 1890, following a bitter crisis, William II forced Bismarck's resignation. The king was overjoyed. He was at last sole ruler, "master of both big and little matters" (to quote his own words).

In that very same year, 1890, in the valley of 'Akká, in the Holy Land, the place described by Hosea as a "door of hope" for mankind, the Prisoner received a visit from a well-known British scholar, Professor Edward Granville Browne of Cambridge University.

During that interview, the Prisoner spoke of just such "ruinous wars" as the kaiser was contemplating. He spoke of the "fruitless strifes" that plagued Europe and the world. The Prisoner said, "We see your kings and rulers lavishing their treasures more freely on means for the destruction of the human race than on that which would conduce to the happiness of mankind."[10]

No greater challenge to the views of Kaiser William II could be found than these words spoken by the Prisoner to Professor Browne on that occasion: "Let not a man glory in this that he loves his country; let him rather glory in this, that he loves his kind."[11]

While the kaiser was plotting the conquest of his neighbors by force, the Prisoner was reemphasizing His words of unity and peace. He told Professor Browne:

Thou hast come to see a prisoner and an exile. . . . We desire but the good of the world and the happiness of the nations; yet they deem us a stirrer-up of strife and sedition worthy of bondage and banishment. . . . That all nations should become one in faith and all men as brothers; that the bonds of affection and unity between the sons of men should be strengthened; that the diversity of religion should cease, and differences of race be annulled—what harm is there in this? . . . Yet so it shall be; these fruitless strifes, these ruinous wars shall pass away, and the "Most Great Peace" shall come. . . . Do not you in Europe need this also?[12]

Meanwhile, in Europe, Kaiser William II of Germany rejoiced at the downfall of his chancellor, Bismarck.

There were no longer any restraints upon the kaiser. He announced exultantly that the course remained as it was—full steam ahead!

The scourge of Europe.

Disaster Course

It was a disaster course.

The fate predicted by the Prisoner for all such unjust kings was soon to overtake the entire Hohenzollern dynasty. It struck initially at the emperor to whom the Prisoner had written his first dire warnings. Later, it engulfed his successor, Kaiser William II, and abolished their rule forever.

William I sustained three attempts on his life. Although he recovered, he lived in constant fear of renewed attacks until his death. His peace of mind was gone.

It was William II, however, who has to accept the guilt for ushering in the catastrophe that was to dethrone him and his dynasty. It would be naive, of course, to blame the kaiser alone for the advent of World War I. He was but one of many contributing causes. There is, however, no doubt that this was a war for which he longed. It was a war that he schemed to hasten in every way possible. Germany, under his goading, constantly demonstrated its military might to the world, until at last the first blow was struck.

The might of the Kaiser's armies was immediately victorious on almost every front. His early triumphs appeared to have overpowered his adversaries. There seemed little doubt that Germany would have a quick and conclusive victory.

The news of these resounding triumphs flashed around the world. Stories of the German victories found a very welcome reception in certain quarters of Persia, the Prisoner's homeland. These easy and astonishing successes of the advancing army of Kaiser William II led to the ridicule of the Prisoner and His Faith.

The Prisoner had written, "O banks of the Rhine! We have seen you covered with gore, inasmuch as the swords of retribution were drawn against you; and you shall have another turn."[13]

The Prisoner warned the emperor of Germany of the fate that would overtake his nation and capital city if the king followed in the foolish footsteps of Napoleon III, who had already gone "down to dust."

Bahá'u'lláh had written, "Think deeply, O King. . . . Be warned, be of them who reflect. . . . We hear the lamentations of Berlin, though she be today in conspicuous glory."[14]

The kaiser and the world may have paid little attention to the Prisoner's prophecies about Germany, but his enemies in Persia had *not* forgotten. This was their hour of delight.

The news spread rapidly. It was too good to keep: "His great prophecy about Germany has proved to be false!"

"Where are the lamentations of Berlin?"

"Are the banks of the Rhine covered with blood?"

"Has Germany had even *one* turn, let alone a second?"

The devoted followers of the Prisoner remained silent as the German army advanced. What could they say? The Prisoner's ominous words about Germany *had* remained unfulfilled. The Rhine had *not* been a scene of slaughter. Instead, Berlin was in "conspicuous glory."

Exactly the opposite of what the Prisoner had prophesied was taking place in Germany. The kaiser was sweeping all before him. In many quarters, the might of the kaiser's armies was considered to be well-nigh invincible.

The magnificently trained divisions of the German High Command became the scourge of Europe. Under the banner of *"Gott mit uns!"* ("God is with us") they rolled over all opposition. They delighted their friends and terrified their enemies. They were making a laughingstock of the Prisoner's predictions.

God did indeed appear to be with the kaiser.

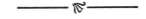

The teeth of the tiger are drawn,
and he is banished forever.

The Inglorious Exit

The tragic events that succeeded these early triumphs proved that the Prisoner's words had been no idle prediction.

Every beholder with "eyes to see" was soon to gaze upon the awesome fulfillment of every one of His pronouncements. The consequences, long delayed, were all the more severe.

The Prisoner had written, for all who doubted the potency of God to achieve His ends, "Dost thou believe thou hast the power to frustrate His Will, to hinder Him from executing His judgment, or to deter Him from exercising His sovereignty? Pretendest thou that aught in the heavens or in the earth can resist His Faith? No, by Him Who is the Eternal Truth! Nothing whatsoever in the whole of creation can thwart His Purpose."[15]

Those words soon came true.

The war, which had begun so impressively for Germany, suddenly soured on every front. Unforeseen reverses, swift and fatal, overtook the kaiser and all his armies. Suddenly, the war was lost.

The "terms of a treaty notorious in its severity" crushed the life out of the German people. It shrouded their hopes for the future. The "lamentations of Berlin" were heard on every side.

The Prisoner's enemies in Persia now bitterly regretted having called attention to those fate-laden words contained in His prophecies.

Even more remarkable than the "lamentations of Berlin" was the promise that the Prisoner had directed to the banks of the Rhine. Because of its aggressive military policy, Germany suffered not *once*, but *twice*. She was crushed in both world wars.

Two times the banks of the Rhine were "covered with gore." Twice the "lamentations" were heard around the world. The German nation did have "another turn," when not only the "swords of retribution" were raised against her a second time, but bombs as well. Nations shattered the Nazi empire of Adolph Hitler, leveling many parts of the capital city, Berlin.[16]

On November 11, 1918, newspaper headlines in Berlin flashed the news: "Kaiser abdicates!"

The dumbfounded and war-weary emperor had not yet even been informed. On Sunday, November 10, one day before the armistice, William II had fled ignominiously to Holland, his train slipping quietly away from the station at Spa into the early morning fog.

The kaiser transferred to an automobile at the Dutch border. It must have been a humiliating experience. Not only had his armies surrendered, but there, at Dutch customs, the kaiser had to surrender his sword to the customs officer. The teeth of the tiger had been drawn, and he was banished from his homeland forever, exactly as the Prisoner had been banished.

Taylor, in his history, states, "There have been more tragic and more disgraceful exits from the stage of history, but few more inglorious."[17]

God promised to destroy the king and the princes.

The Second Kingdom Falls

The Hohenzollern dynasty passed away. With it vanished many of their fellow kings and princes. Before November 15, 1918, the princes of all the German states had abdicated, and all other contemporary German thrones had fallen. The king, the crown prince, and all the lesser princes of Germany were removed completely and permanently from their places of honor.

The empire of the Hohenzollerns toppled to the dust. Its official death-knell was sounded November 28, 1918, when William II signed a formal act of abdication, which ended his rule both as Prussian king and German emperor.

This document brought to an end the 250-year reign of oppression by the powerful Hohenzollern dynasty. The constitution that followed swept away forever the German monarchy. It carried into oblivion with it all the imperial princes, and scattered forever all the lesser kings of German states, along with their attendant princes.

Around the world, clergymen saw in these cataclysmic events the fulfillment of Biblical prophecies. But the truth is far greater than any of them grasped. The prophet Jeremiah, speaking of the latter days, said that God promised, "And I will set my throne in Elam [Persia], and will destroy from thence the king and the princes."[18]

The Prisoner had come from Persia, which Jeremiah called Elam, and He had already delivered the commands whose rejection had led to the destruction of the kings and princes of two great nations.

The entire story of Bahá'u'lláh has its roots deep in the scriptures of all the great religions. In the fate of the other monarchs to whom Bahá'u'lláh directed His appeal was to be the fulfillment of even more remarkable promises and warnings.

In Germany, the second kingdom had fallen.

5 ❧ THE THIRD KINGDOM FALLS

One of thy ministers extended Me his aid.

The Czar-Liberator

No other chapter in the story of the Prisoner and the kings has such elements of classic tragedy as that concerning Russia and its unhappy monarch, Alexander II. It is difficult to feel much sympathy for the emperor of France, the vain and vulgar Louis Napoleon. It is nearly impossible to feel it for the Hohenzollern kaisers, whose arrogance played so great a role in dragging humankind into the horrors of World War I.

It is not difficult to feel sympathy, on the other hand, for a man whose weakness and timidity led him into fatal errors. All of us on occasion feel weak and timid. Unhappily, however, those who accept positions of great trust and power, and who derive the benefits of such position, also must accept its obligations. The only alternative is to surrender the position and retire to a less demanding role in human affairs.

Alexander II was in many respects a remarkable man. He was certainly a most unusual czar. With few exceptions his predecessors had been hard, brutal autocrats ruling their vast domain with an iron fist. One of the most famous, Peter the Great, had killed his own son. Another, the notorious "Ivan the Terrible," had literally bricked his enemies up alive in the walls of the Kremlin.

Alexander was repelled by this family history. He was essentially a good-natured and compassionate man who abhorred suffering. Further, unlike other members of the Romanov family, he had been educated by a French tutor. As a result, he had adopted a number of very liberal and progressive ideas.

To many, his accession was hailed as the dawn of a new day. Russia's greatest social problem was the serfdom of those who toiled in misery on the estates of the great lords. The second most urgent problem was the lack of anything like democratic government.

Alexander was known to favor extensive reforms in both these areas. Relatively early in his reign he astonished the world and alarmed the aristocracy by abolishing serfdom throughout Russia. This was four years before the United States abolished the even worse institution of Negro slavery. Alexander followed this progressive act with others designed to begin a gradual and more equitable distribution of land, so that peasants could own their own farms and have a voice in government. The millennium appeared to be on its way in Russia. Alexander was hailed as the "czar-liberator."

It was to this remarkable emperor that Bahá'u'lláh addressed one of His most loving and moving appeals. The Russian government had already shown its potentiality for good some years earlier when its minister was the one major foreign figure in Ṭihrán to intervene directly on behalf of the persecuted Prisoner of Náṣiri'd-Dín Sháh. The consul addressed the court openly, denouncing what he called "the absurd falsity" of the charges against Bahá'u'lláh.

Subsequently, upon Bahá'u'lláh's release and exile, a Russian official accompanied the party as far as the Turkish border. Without doubt, such intervention was both a comfort and an aid to the little band of exiles. Bahá'u'lláh foretold a great station for the czar if he would in like manner try to help humanity.

Bahá'u'lláh directed these words to Alexander: "Whilst I lay, chained and fettered, in the prison . . . [in Persia], one of thy ministers extended Me his aid. Wherefore hath God ordained for thee a station which the knowledge of none can comprehend."[1]

The place of prestige would not be automatically conferred. The czar would have to labor industriously to attain it. He would have to be of service to his fellow man, and exert his efforts to bring the hearts of men back to God, and to acquaint the world with the message of unity and justice that Bahá'u'lláh brought.

But God would help him—Bahá'u'lláh assured Alexander: "Thy Lord is, in truth, potent over all things. He giveth what He willeth to whomsoever He willeth."[2]

Would the czar-liberator listen?

How great hath been My patience.

Hearken Unto the Voice

Bahá'u'lláh called upon Alexander II to take the leadership in raising the moral and ethical standards of men: "O Czar of Russia. . . . Arise thou amongst men in the name of this all-compelling Cause, and summon, then, the nations unto God."[3]

Bahá'u'lláh told the czar that there was no refuge for any man in this day save in God. "He, verily, ordaineth what He pleaseth. Thy Lord truly preserveth whom He willeth, be he in the midst of the seas, or in the maw of the serpent, or beneath the sword of the oppressor."[4]

In that same letter, Bahá'u'lláh said that He had heard the wishes that the czar had spoken secretly in his heart in prayer. Bahá'u'lláh promised Alexander that God was willing to grant the king his desire if he in turn would be faithful to his trust as a true king. Bahá'u'lláh declared, "We, verily, have heard the thing for which thou didst supplicate thy Lord, whilst secretly communing with Him. Wherefore, the breeze of My loving-kindness wafted forth, and the sea of My mercy surged, and We answered thee in truth."[5]

It was as though the Emperor Tiberius Caesar received a promise from Christ that if he would accept His message and proclaim it, Caesar would be the envy of the past, present, and future. It was a promise similar to that which Bahá'u'lláh had offered to Napoleon III, who had refused it and had fallen from his high place.

Thus, for a moment, Czar Alexander II Nicolaevich was at the threshold of a greatness unrivaled in the recorded history of royalty. He could have had the support and guidance of a Messenger of God in his actions. Alexander only needed to stretch forth his hand in help to the Promised One Whose coming had glorified the pages of the czar's own sacred scriptures.

Eager that the king should understand this and not miss his golden opportunity, Bahá'u'lláh repeated His entreaty: "Again I say, Hearken unto My Voice that calleth from My prison. . . . that thou mayest perceive how great hath been My patience."[6]

Bahá'u'lláh foresaw an unrivaled position for the czar. The king needed to take but one step to make it a reality.

Bahá'u'lláh wrote, "O Czar of Russia. . . . By My Life! Couldst thou but know the things sent down by My Pen, and discover the treasures of My Cause . . . thou wouldst, in thy love for My name, and in thy longing for My glorious and sublime Kingdom, lay down thy life in My path. . . . Blessed be the king whose sovereignty hath withheld him not from his Sovereign, and who hath turned unto God with his heart."[7]

Certainly Alexander needed such reassurances, as his reforms had engulfed him in trouble. On the one hand, the nobility and clergy were violently opposed to his policies, which would cost them land and influence. They undermined the czar in every way they could. On the other, a new generation of revolutionaries who believed in nothing but terrorism had arisen. They felt confident that the czar would fail. They could see no way in which he could ever hope to mobilize the mass of the ignorant and superstitious peasantry behind his throne. The peasants loved the czar, but they understood nothing and were entirely disorganized. The terrorists waited expectantly for the moment they could launch a national revolution.

Alexander became desperate. The one powerful group on whom he had relied were intellectuals in the government and the schools. These men, however, saw in the situation only a chance to make their personal reputations. They quarreled among themselves for position and influence.

The czar realized that his program was built on shifting sands. Where could he find the moral and spiritual force that would enlist the mass of the Russian people in the cause of social change? The people were intensely religious, and social reform (he thought) had no religious content at all. Religion, the only power that could move Russia's millions, seemed irrelevant. Certainly the religion of the Orthodox Church was little more than a mass of crusted superstitions and rituals.

There is no more tragic and ironic story in history. At the very point in time that a spiritual authority for social change was desperately needed, that authority had been given. Christianity and the earlier religious revelations had been addressed to individuals. Now, through Bahá'u'lláh, God was speaking to nations, economic classes, racial groups, and institutions. And He was speaking on the very problems that were convulsing the world.

It is impossible to imagine the effect that would have ensued in Russia had the czar, "the little father of the people," the deeply trusted head of Russia's vast family and of the church itself, announced the return of Christ and the inauguration of the kingdom of unity and justice. Nothing could have stood in his way.

Alexander hesitated, vacillated, and then decided. He ignored the message of the Prisoner of 'Akká and gave in to the pressures of his nobles. He had waded into the stream and now staggered fearfully back to the familiar shore.

The words of Bahá'u'lláh to the czar ring in our ears: "Couldst thou . . . discover the treasures of My Cause . . . thou wouldst, in thy love for My Name, and in thy longing for My glorious and sublime Kingdom, lay down thy life in My path."[8]

A great trembling seized and
rocked the foundations of that country.

The Third Kingdom Falls

The House of Romanov fell, as had the Houses of Napoleon and Hohenzollern. Its fortunes declined with progressive swiftness until World War I. Bolshevism arose during that fiery upheaval, shook the throne of the czars, and then abolished it.

The last years of the reign of Alexander II were given over to terrorism and unexampled violence. Alexander reversed his liberal policies and inaugurated a program of repression that was taken up and expanded by his two autocratic successors. The czar lived in fear of his life. Living itself became a daily ordeal. Alexander would not leave the palace except under heavy guard. He preferred not to leave at all. He ordered his quarters to be searched carefully each night before retiring for fear of concealed assassins.

On March 13, 1881, the czar was riding in his carriage along one of the central streets of St. Petersburg near the Winter Palace. The fatal day had arrived at last. A series of small bombs was exploded in his path. His vehicle overturned, and the blast shredded the king's carriage. Alexander survived, and was questioning the would-be assassin when the latter's accomplice threw another bomb directly in front of the czar's feet. Alexander died a few hours later in his room at the royal palace.

The next Romanov, Alexander III, was cut from a more tyrannical pattern, and his successor Nicholas II—the last of the czars—was equally rigid but, unhappily for him, far less able.

What had been a general growing discontent among the masses now became an organized revolt. Both intellectuals and peasants arose against the czar. Their hatred finally erupted in the midst of World War I as the flame of revolution swept across the land—a revolution unparalleled in modern history. It challenged all age-old principles. It upended ancient and time-honored institutions and spread havoc, destruction and death on every side. The death-throes of the Romanov dynasty have been described in these words:

A great trembling seized and rocked the foundations of that country. The light of religion was dimmed. Ecclesiastical institutions of every denomination were swept away. The state religion was disendowed, persecuted and abolished. A far-flung empire was dismembered. A militant, triumphant proletariat exiled the intellectuals, and plundered and massacred the nobility. Civil war and disease decimated a population, already in the throes of agony and despair. And, finally, the Chief Magistrate of a mighty dominion, together with his consort, and his family, and his dynasty, were swept into the vortex of this great convulsion and perished.[9]

This brought to an end the line of kings that had ruled Russia for three hundred years. They, too, had turned a deaf ear to the words of the Messenger of God: "O ye rulers of the earth! . . . Hearken unto the counsel given you by the Pen of the Most High, that haply both ye and the poor may attain unto tranquility and peace. We beseech God to assist the kings of the earth to establish peace on earth. . . . Beware lest ye disregard the counsel of the All-Knowing, the Faithful."[10]

The House of Romanov collapsed, and the dynasty of which Alexander Nicolaevitch II had been so proud came to an end. The czars had not "stayed the hand of the oppressors," nor had they "safeguarded the rights of the downtrodden." In the wake of this disaster, every prophecy that Bahá'u'lláh, the "Glory of God," had uttered concerning the fate of oppressive monarchs had been fulfilled.

When we look back over this tragic history and the failure of faith that set it in motion, Bahá'u'lláh's words to Alexander II and through him to the government of Russia seem among the most poignant that He wrote: "Beware lest thy desire deter thee from turning toward the face of thy Lord. . . . Beware lest thou barter away this sublime station. . . . Beware lest thy sovereignty withhold thee from the Supreme Sovereign."[11]

And how relevant to the Romanov tragedy and its unhappy inaugurator, Alexander, seem the words of the Old Testament prophet Haggai concerning this day: "I will shake all nations, and the desire of all nations shall come: and I will fill this house with glory, saith the Lord of hosts. . . . I will overthrow the throne of kingdoms . . . and I will overthrow the chariots, and those that ride in them."[12]

The third kingdom had fallen.

6 ❧ THE FOURTH KINGDOM FALLS

We have found thee clinging to the Branch,
and heedless of the Root.

The End of the Holy Roman Empire

"The Empire of the Hapsburgs disintegrate and disappear from the face of the earth entirely? Never! There has always been an Empire as long as Europe itself has existed."

These might have been the words of any observer in Europe during those days in which Bahá'u'lláh addressed a special message to Franz Josef, the autocratic ruler of the Austro-Hungarian monarchy.

It would vanish as a mist before the rising sun.

Who could believe such a thing about the Holy Roman Empire? The empire had suffered many vicissitudes; it had its problems, some of them very serious. But it held together the entire economic structure of central Europe. The Danube was Europe's highway and marketplace, and the Hapsburg Empire was its protector. No matter how desperate conditions got, its subject peoples would not bite off their noses to spite their imperial faces. Yet the empire did vanish, "like a mist," and it vanished overnight.

Emperor Franz Josef journeyed to the Holy Land to pay tribute to Christ. He passed within a short distance of the prison in which Bahá'u'lláh was being held captive.

The prison city of 'Akká, called Acco in ancient times, is a site referred to by Hosea, who had prophesied that it would be a "door of hope" for mankind. Isaiah prophesied that this city would be a "place for the herds" of the flock of the Lord, "for my people that have sought me."

Franz Josef did not seek out Bahá'u'lláh nor inquire concerning Him, despite the reputation as a reformer and saint that Bahá'u'lláh's life had won among European writers and diplomats.

From that prison-city Bahá'u'lláh addressed His historic words to Franz Josef: "O Emperor of Austria! He Who is the Dayspring of God's Light dwelt in the prison of 'Akká, at the time when thou didst set forth to visit the Aqsá Mosque [in Jerusalem]. Thou passed Him by, and inquired not about Him, by Whom every house is exalted, and every lofty gate unlocked. We, verily, made it a place whereunto the world should turn, that they might remember Me, and yet thou hast rejected Him Who is the Object of this remembrance."[1]

The first reaction of almost anyone who had not investigated Bahá'u'lláh's Faith might be to say, "Who could blame the emperor? If I were king and anyone spoke such words as those to me, I would ignore them. Such a claim is preposterous."

Yet an answer like this is not possible for anyone who really believes in one of the world religions. Christians, Jews, Muslims are people who believe that God does speak through Messengers and that His Messengers have always made the same kind of announcement. These Messengers have always been persecuted, and God has promised to send One, in the fullness of time, who will be a "Prince of Peace." The Christian church is based on exactly that same "preposterous" claim by a so-called madman Who was too "weak" to save Himself. Christ's words were also branded as false in His day.

Franz Joseph believed that. He heard Mass every day. Every day he listened to the familiar story of Jesus, Who had been rejected by Herod and Pilate. Every day, he appealed to God to keep His promise, "Thy will be done, on earth."

The problem with promises given us by God, as the Pharisees found two thousand years ago, is that, inevitably, God will keep them.

To Franz Joseph, Bahá'u'lláh wrote, "We have . . . found thee clinging unto the Branch and heedless of the Root."[2]

———— ❧ ————

We have come to unite and weld together all who dwell on earth.

Break in Pieces

The royal visit of Emperor Franz Josef to the Holy Land was one of pomp and ceremony. The cost of such pageantry throughout his empire of drones and princes was sustained by the labor and sacrifices of the neglected people of his realm.

Franz Josef, like his fellow monarchs, was heedless of Bahá'u'lláh's words: "Know ye that the poor are the trust of God in your midst. Watch that ye betray not His trust, that ye deal not unjustly with them and that ye walk not in the ways of the treacherous."[3]

Bahá'u'lláh must have been sorrowed by the conduct of the emperor, who came so near the object of his keenest desire. Yet His sorrow was even greater for humanity.

He comforted the downtrodden, saying that even if every ruler opposed the Revelation of God, this would sooner or later bind together all men in a common effort toward a common goal: peace and freedom. The leaders of men could either hasten or delay its fulfillment, but they would be powerless to stop it.

From the prison-city of 'Akká, Bahá'u'lláh wrote, "We, verily, have come to unite and weld together all that dwell on earth. Unto this beareth witness what the ocean of Mine utterance hath revealed amongst men, and yet most of the people have gone astray."[4]

He had "come to the Holy Land" from the "east" by "way of the gate" as foretold in those passages of scripture honored by the emperor of the Holy Roman Empire. Franz Josef, one of the most powerful monarchs of that era, brushed shoulders with the Prisoner of 'Akká, yet was still oblivious of His words to the leaders of men: "It is incumbent upon thee to summon the people, under all conditions, to whatever will cause them to show forth spiritual characteristics and goodly deeds, so that all may become aware of that which is the cause of human upliftment."[5]

Bahá'u'lláh, a prisoner, could not visit Europe, but the emperor of Austria came to the Holy Land and passed under His shadow. They were not destined to meet. Bahá'u'lláh's words to Franz Josef were to remain unheeded until history could look back upon their fulfillment.

Bahá'u'lláh declared that the day was approaching when men would "behold the Daystar of justice shining in its full splendor" and no one could prevent its "shining." He wrote, "Who is there that can put out the light which the snow-white Hand of God hath lit? Where is he to be found that hath the power to quench the fire which hath been kindled through the might of thy Lord?"[6]

Certainly no king would be able to prevent the rise and spread of His Faith or to dim the light He had ignited in the hearts of His followers. Bahá'u'lláh Himself wrote, "The fierce gales and whirlwinds of the world and its peoples can never shake the foundation upon which the rock-like stability of My chosen ones is based."[7]

"Thus instructeth thee" the Messenger of God for this day from the "grievous Prison." Neither kings nor peoples could hold back the rising sun of His teachings. They were God-directed for the betterment of all humankind. Bahá'u'lláh wrote, "Members of the human race! Hold ye fast by the Cord which no man can sever. This will, indeed, profit you all the days of your life, for its strength is of God, the Lord of all worlds. . . . Though encompassed with a myriad griefs and afflictions, We have, with mighty confidence, summoned the peoples of the earth. . . . This Holy Land hath been mentioned and extolled in all the sacred Scriptures. . . . Whatever hath come to pass in this Day hath been foretold in the Scriptures of old."[8]

Jeremiah, speaking of the great One Who would come from Persia in "that day" to destroy "the king and the princes" also foreshadowed the fate of those nations that opposed Him: "Thou art my battle axe and weapons of war: for with thee I will break in pieces the nations, and with thee will I destroy kingdoms."[9]

The fall of the fourth kingdom was under way. No nation, no empire, was to "break in pieces" in such a dramatic and permanent fashion as that of the kingdom of the Hapsburgs.

Ye, and all ye possess, shall pass away.

The Fourth Kingdom Falls

The rumblings of an internal disintegration heralded the earthquake that threatened the kingdom of Franz Josef.

Bahá'u'lláh's counsel to the kings of the earth concerning the rights of their subjects was this: "Shouldst thou cause rivers of justice to spread their waters amongst thy subjects, God would surely aid thee with the hosts of the unseen and of the seen, and would strengthen thee in thine affairs."[10]

The actions of the emperor of Austria-Hungary were directly opposite. Rivers of justice did not "flow" through the land, and Franz Josef was neither "aided" nor "strengthened" in the deepening crises that began to engulf his rambling empire in the late nineteenth century.

The fate that awaited such kings was described in these words by Bahá'u'lláh: "Ye continue roving with delight in the valley of your corrupt desires. Ye, and all ye possess, shall pass away."[11]

It has been said of the rule of Franz Josef that "repeated tragedies darkened his reign."[12] Calamitous events succeeded one another with alarming persistence.

His brother, Maximilian, was defeated, imprisoned, and shot to death by a peasant revolution in Mexico. His son, Crown Prince Rudolph, disgraced the royal family and finally perished in a dishonorable affair. His wife, Empress Elizabeth, was assassinated in Geneva. The archduke Francis Ferdinand and his wife were struck down by assassins in Sarajevo. This very tragedy was the spark that ignited the great world war. Shortly after, Franz Josef himself succumbed to death.

The death of the emperor brought to a close a reign "unsurpassed by any other reign in the disasters it brought to the nation." Composed of conglomerate states, races, and languages, the Holy Roman Empire relentlessly began to disintegrate. "All that was left of the once formidable Holy Roman Empire was a shrunken republic that led a miserable existence."[13] The tiny Austrian republic was taken over by Hitler and restored in 1945 as the uneasy meeting ground of four armies of occupation.

The words of Bahá'u'lláh echoed from His prison cell in the Holy Land out across the Mediterranean Sea. They found their dire fulfillment in the overthrow of the dynasty of the Hapsburgs, sweeping away both king and princes alike.

The Hapsburgs, like their fellow monarchs, punished themselves by wrong decisions. The first error, the rejection of the Messenger of God, was spiritual. Moral errors followed in such areas of concern as peace and justice. Finally, very obvious political miscalculations completed the work. Forgetful of both God and man, men of power seek to exalt their own position, party or nation; and, as this is contrary to the spirit of justice and love, they bring about their own downfall—some rapidly, some slowly, all inevitably.

The Messenger of God is the lawgiver for His day. Those who break the laws pay the penalty. In secular society, those who ignore or break the established laws suffer the consequences of their own neglect. These outer laws are a mirror of the realm of the moral, ethical, and spiritual Laws of God that are the foundation and basis of all life on earth. Therefore the punishment is more severe and is worldwide, as the offenders are both the leaders and the people of the earth.

When the sun rises, all life on the planet must adjust itself to the new day. Flowers open their blossoms to the gradually warming sunlight. Should the blossoms neglect to open until the noonday sun beats down upon them, they would be destroyed.

In like manner, kingdoms and peoples that have refused for over a century to open their hearts to the Sun of truth for this Day, Bahá'u'lláh, promised throughout their own holy books, now find themselves endangered through their refusal to adjust to the light and heat of a new Day.

The new springtime came with the birth of the Bahá'í Faith in 1844. The spring has come and passed. The icy indifference and cold snows of opposition should have melted ages ago; now this glacial-like neglect is powerless to resist the summer-heat of the Sun of Bahá'u'lláh's teachings. Helpless before the blazing rays, it melts and floods, and sweeps away all before it.

How startling and apt appear the words of the prophet Zephaniah when we consider the fate of Emperor Franz Josef and his family. Zephaniah prophesied the coming of "the great day of the Lord" when the Lord would be in His "holy mountain."

Franz Josef visited that mountain and, as we have seen, passed within the shadow of the prison of 'Akká. In Bahá'u'lláh's own words, the Emperor had not even "inquired" about Him.

Now the king and the princes of the royal House of Hapsburg were no more. Such a time had been envisioned by the prophet Zephaniah, who said, "I will also stretch out mine hand upon . . . them that are turned back from the Lord; and those that have not sought the Lord, nor inquired for him. . . . And it shall come to pass in the day of the Lord's sacrifice, that I will punish the princes, and the king's children."[14]

The fourth kingdom had fallen.

7 ❧ A KINGDOM STANDS

If this is of God, it will endure.

A Kingdom Stands

"O Queen in London! Incline thine ear unto the voice of thy Lord. . . . All that hath been mentioned in the Gospel hath been fulfilled."[1]

Bahá'u'lláh addressed these words to Queen Victoria of Great Britain. In His letter to the queen, Bahá'u'lláh once again linked His Message with that of Christ. He said that the city of 'Akká had been "honored by the footsteps" of the Promised One.[2]

In this day, Bahá'u'lláh said, the people of the world had the opportunity to "inhale the fragrance" of the Revelation of God, and to become "inebriated with the wine of His [the Messenger's] presence."[3]

Bahá'u'lláh praised Queen Victoria for two far-reaching reforms undertaken by the British government. He wrote, "We have been informed that thou hast forbidden the trading in slaves. . . . This, verily, is what God hath enjoined in this wondrous Revelation. God hath, truly, destined a reward for thee, because of this. He, verily, will pay the doer of good, whether man or woman, his due recompense."[4]

In yet another part of His letter to the queen, Bahá'u'lláh said, "Thou hast entrusted the reins of counsel into the hands of the representatives of the people. Thou, indeed, hast done well, for thereby the foundations of the edifice of thine affairs will be strengthened, and the hearts of all that are beneath thy shadow, whether high or low, will be tranquilized."[5]

Bahá'u'lláh deplored the state of the world. He longed to see mankind at peace, developing the creative talents of every heart. Bahá'u'lláh attributed much of man's suffering to the insincerity and greed of political leaders.

He wrote, "We behold it [the world], in this day, at the mercy of rulers so drunk with pride that they cannot discern clearly their own best advantage, much less recognize a Revelation so bewildering and challenging as this. And whenever any one of them [leaders] hath striven to improve its condition, his motive hath been his own gain, whether confessedly so or not; and the unworthiness of this motive hath limited his power to heal or cure."[6]

Bahá'u'lláh prescribed the remedy that could heal the ills of the world: "O Queen in London. . . . That which the Lord hath ordained as the sovereign remedy and mightiest instrument for the healing of all the world is the union of all its peoples in one universal Cause, one common Faith. This can in no wise be achieved except through the power of a skilled, an all-powerful and inspired Physician."[7]

In what spirit did the queen receive Bahá'u'lláh's letter? According to one written account: "Queen Victoria, it is said, upon reading the Tablet [letter] revealed for her, remarked: 'If this is of God, it will endure.'"[8]

Like Gamaliel, the leading rabbi who refused either to condemn Christ or to accept Him, the queen preferred to leave history to take its course.

Of all the rulers to whom Bahá'u'lláh wrote, Victoria was the only one who responded in any manner, however limited. She is also the only one of those monarchs who did not undergo a series of afflictive dynasty-destroying disasters during her reign, and whose kingdom has survived.

Queen Victoria died on January 22, 1901, during the South African Boer War. She had ruled her people for over sixty-three years, the longest reign known in British history. Victoria had indeed been blessed with a reign that was in sharp contrast with those of her fellow rulers.

There was, however, to be a far more direct link between the queen and the Prisoner. An even greater "reward" was to come to one of Victoria's descendants.

The queen's granddaughter, Queen Marie of Romania, subsequently became a devoted follower of the Prisoner of 'Akká. Several testimonies to Bahá'u'lláh's Faith have been left by the pen of this royal convert. Publicly the queen proclaimed, "If ever the name of Bahá'u'lláh . . . comes to your attention, do not put [His] writings from you. . . . Let their glorious, peace-bringing, love-creating lessons sink into your hearts as they have into mine. . . . Seek them and be the happier."[9]

She later wrote, "It is Christ's message taken up anew, in the same words almost, but adapted to the thousand years and more difference that lies between the year one and today."[10]

Canadian Bahá'ís were delighted that it was in a letter to a Canadian newspaper, the *Toronto Star,* that the queen's public declaration was first made.

There is also a second link between Queen Marie, the first member of royalty to embrace the Faith of Bahá'u'lláh, and the kings to whom Bahá'u'lláh directed specific letters. Queen Marie of Romania was the granddaughter of both Queen Victoria and Alexander II of Russia. Victoria was the sole monarch to make even the slightest response to Bahá'u'lláh's message. Although Alexander II was himself indifferent, it was one of his ministers who made an effort, however futile, to rescue Bahá'u'lláh from His persecutors.

The granddaughter of these two monarchs was the first of the line of kings to recognize and accept the mission of

Bahá'u'lláh, a mission that its author stated would eventually secure the allegiance of most of the human race.

What blessings would have come to the nation whose ruler had truly heeded the words that Bahá'u'lláh addressed to them? What blessings would have come to all humankind?

Bahá'u'lláh Himself promised, "How great is the blessedness that awaiteth the king who will arise to aid My Cause in My Kingdom, who will detach himself from all else but Me!"[11]

Bahá'u'lláh told one of the kings that if it had not been for the "repudiation" of the religious leaders and the conspiracy of the rulers, He would have given them guidance that would have "thrilled and carried away the hearts"—guidance that would "cheer the eyes" and "tranquilize the souls" of men.

Bahá'u'lláh severely censured those kings who refused to make any effort to investigate the truth of His Faith. Their failure was reflected and repeated in their neglect of their responsibility to God for the welfare of their people and the peace of the world.

We should not, however, make the mistake of thinking that this condemnation represented a criticism of kingship itself. Much less can it be regarded as an attack on established government.

Bahá'u'lláh foretold the day when just kings and other rulers would arise and seize the opportunity that earlier leaders had so tragically missed. Bahá'u'lláh wrote, "Erelong will God make manifest on earth kings who will recline on the couches of justice, and will rule amongst men even as they rule their own selves. They, indeed, are among the choicest of My creatures in the entire creation."[12]

Bahá'u'lláh described the blessing that such leadership would bring to the entire planet:

O concourse of the rulers of the world! There is no force on earth that can equal in its conquering power the force of justice and wisdom . . . Blessed is the king who marcheth with the ensign of wisdom unfurled before him, and the battalions of justice massed in his rear. He verily is the ornament that adorneth the brow of peace and the countenance of security. There can be no doubt whatever that if the daystar of justice, which the clouds of tyranny have obscured, were to shed its light upon men, the face of the earth would be completely transformed.[13]

In Queen Victoria's case, we are so familiar with the halo of respect surrounding her and her throne that we are in danger of overlooking an important historical fact, one that has far-ranging implications for our story.

When Victoria ascended the throne in 1838, the British monarchy was at the lowest ebb in its history. Her grandfather George III had been insane. Her uncle George IV was a national disgrace, the inspiration for the vulgar nursery rhyme "Georgie Porgie." Her immediate predecessor, her second uncle, William IV, was publicly mocked during his lifetime, and on the day of his funeral was described by the *London Times* as "only a common sort of person."

Victoria was a young, inexperienced woman, the last member of a junior branch of the family. She appeared to have little to commend her. It was common knowledge in London that she would be the last British monarch and that Britain would follow France, the United States and other "progressive" nations in establishing a republic.

In fact, Victoria was to rule for sixty years and leave the monarchy more secure than it had ever been in its history!

Bahá'u'lláh clearly indicated that even the slightest response to God's call would bring very great blessings. The tiniest ray of light penetrating the camera lens can imprint upon the receptive film an entire picture. The mind is staggered at the potential that could be released by a mass response to the divine summons.

Unlike Queen Victoria and her government, the other European monarchs had been far removed from the will of God. They had experienced the full effect of their neglect of their trust and the irrelevancy of their pursuits.

The nineteenth-century monarchs who were the exact antithesis of Bahá'u'lláh's teachings, however, were the kings of Persia and Turkey.

They not only failed to make the slightest response to Bahá'u'lláh's words, but actively joined forces repeatedly to persecute, imprison, and exile the Messenger of God. Within one of these two empires, over twenty thousand of the early followers of the Bahá'í Faith were slain in the most barbarous fashion.

These next two kings were described by Bahá'u'lláh, one as "the Prince of Oppressors," the other as occupying the "Throne of Tyranny."

He said that God would make them "an object lesson for the world."[14]

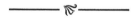

8 ❧ THE EXILE

A wholesale massacre!

The Ruined House

In considering the encounter between the Messenger of God and the rulers of the leading Western nations, we have skipped ahead of events in the Near East. Before going on to the story of the fifth kingdom, let us glance quickly back at these events, which brought Bahá'u'lláh out of His native land and prepared the way for His announcement to the kings.

Bahá'u'lláh was still imprisoned in Ṭihrán's "Black Pit" when an event occurred that appeared certain to lead to His release. The would-be assassin of Náṣiri'd-Dín Sháh had enlisted the help of a half-demented youth. During the course of the persecutions, these two persons were arrested, and the former finally confessed his guilt. He alone had been involved from the beginning, and his only helper had been his pathetic companion.

As soon as the confession was obtained, a representative of the prime minister went immediately to take down the words of that confession. The Russian ministry seized the opportunity to send its translator along because of its interest in the Prisoner. The confession, therefore, received impressive authentication.

Bahá'u'lláh's enemies were enraged. The thought that Bahá'u'lláh might escape from the dungeon when He had been so close to the grave infuriated them.

Before Bahá'u'lláh was released, these conspirators besieged the shah with the new plans that they had contrived. They assured the king that they would be able to involve Bahá'u'lláh in grave troubles. They were confident that these intrigues would ensure His death. The shah, pressed by his mother and accustomed to doing as he wished with those he feared, agreed to their schemes.

He summoned the prime minister and told him to send several detachments of soldiers to Bahá'u'lláh's home district of Núr. These soldiers were told that they were being sent to suppress dangerous "disturbers of the peace." It was expected that this sudden assault would generate widespread confusion and perhaps incite opposition from the villagers. The plan was to blame Bahá'u'lláh for these fresh uprisings and then brand Him as an agitator of political revolt. Bahá'u'lláh's summer home was in the village of Tákur, in the district of Núr.

Although the prime minister, as soon as he heard the instructions, knew very well that the plan was directed against Bahá'u'lláh, he did nothing to prevent it.

A detachment of soldiers was placed under the command of an officer named Mírzá Abú-Tálib. As soon as his troops reached the village of Tákur, Mírzá Abú-Tálib told them to prepare for an all-out attack.

The surprised and defenseless people of the village, upon becoming aware of the soldiers' approach, sent representatives to appeal to the officer. They asked him to give them some reason for such an onslaught. Mírzá Abú-Tálib refused to see them. Instead, he sent a curt message: "I am charged by my sovereign to order a wholesale massacre of the men of this village, to capture the women and to confiscate all property."

The soldiers attacked the house of Bahá'u'lláh as their initial act. Bahá'u'lláh had inherited the beautiful summer residence from His father, a minister of the crown, and the building was known to be furnished with objects of great value.

Mírzá Abú-Tálib ordered his men to break open everything and take away the contents. He instructed that what could not be carried away should be burned or demolished. The walls of the rooms were disfigured beyond repair. The beams were torn down, the decorations destroyed, and the house was left in ruins.

From this opening assault, the troops went on to demolish the homes of other people in the village, after which the entire town was set on fire.

This deliberate provocation, premonitory of similar schemes that twentieth-century tyrants were to use on a large scale against peoples they wished to destroy, was expected to incite fierce opposition. It was assumed that Bahá'u'lláh and His supporters would attempt to arouse the district against the government. The uprising would then be crushed, and Bahá'u'lláh condemned for treason.

It is Our purpose . . . to abolish . . . war,
and bloodshed, from the face of the earth.

Out of the Pit

The new conspiracy failed. Bahá'u'lláh and His family showed no inclination to incite opposition to the crown. And now that His innocence was at last made public, the opportunity to discredit and kill Him had passed. His enemies realized to their chagrin that it was no longer possible or wise to hold Bahá'u'lláh a prisoner.

A minister of the crown was sent to summon Bahá'u'lláh from "the Pit." He was ordered to appear before the authorities so that He might be informed of His freedom. The minister, Ḥájí 'Alí, had once been a friend of Bahá'u'lláh. When he saw that foul prison where Bahá'u'lláh had been kept, with its filth and its vermin-infested floor, he was very distressed.

"May Mírzá Áqá Khán be accursed!" he shouted, denouncing the prime minister. But when he looked upon Bahá'u'lláh, Whom he had loved and respected, he burst into tears. Bahá'u'lláh's hair was matted and dirty. His clothes were torn. His shoulders were festered from the chains that had weighed down His neck.

Ḥájí 'Alí wept aloud. He turned to Bahá'u'lláh in great sorrow. "God is my witness," he told Bahá'u'lláh. "I never realized you were being subjected to such treatment."

Ḥájí 'Alí could not bear to look upon the torn and soiled garments in which Bahá'u'lláh was clothed. He took off his own fine cloak and started to place it over Bahá'u'lláh's shoulders, entreating Him to wear it. Since He was a member of one of Persia's oldest noble families, it seemed wrong for Bahá'u'lláh to appear at court in the condition in which the minister had found Him.

Bahá'u'lláh refused. He preferred, He said, to appear before them in the same clothes in which He had been cast into the dungeon. He would wear the garb of a prisoner, a garb that other innocent people still wore.

He knew that the sufferings He and His friends had sustained in the Síyáh-Chál were but a prelude to far greater troubles yet to come. Once the shah and the clergy realized that He was not merely a prominent Bábí, but the One Whom the Báb had foretold, a veritable flood of tribulations would engulf Him from all sides.

Bahá'u'lláh recalled those pregnant months in the Síyáh-Chál when later He sent His letter to Náṣiri'd-Dín Sháh from the prison of 'Akká. He wrote, "O King! I was but a man like others, asleep upon My couch, when lo, the breezes of the All-Glorious were wafted over Me, and taught Me the knowledge of all that hath been. This thing is not from Me, but from One Who is Almighty and All-Knowing [God]. And He bade Me lift up My voice between earth and heaven, and for this there befell Me what hath caused the tears of every man of understanding to flow."[1]

The guards conducted Bahá'u'lláh from the dungeon-prison to the seat of the imperial government, ushered into the presence of the prime minister, Mírzá Áqá Khán.

The conscience of Mírzá Áqá Khán must have been stricken at the sight of Bahá'u'lláh, Whose treatment had been so severe that none who knew Him would now have recognized Him.

The prime minister had failed to redeem his promise to the Báb. He had not protected and safeguarded the Báb's followers. Instead, the leading minister in the land had himself conducted and masterminded a carnage that European historians would describe as "unparalleled." The Austrian military attaché has written, "My pen shrinks in horror in attempting to describe what befell those valiant men and women."[2]

Mírzá Áqá Khán had proved false to his vows to both the Báb and Bahá'u'lláh, but he was still not prepared to face his conscience. Instead, he spoke harshly to Bahá'u'lláh to cover his own shame.

"If you had taken my advice," he told Bahá'u'lláh, "and cut yourself off from the Faith of the Báb, you wouldn't have suffered this agony and indignity."[3]

Bahá'u'lláh looked into his eyes and replied simply, "Had you, in turn, followed My Counsels, the affairs of the government would not have reached so critical a stage."[4]

Who will ever know the thoughts that coursed through the mind of Mírzá Áqá Khán? Did he recall the earlier occasion when, stricken with illness, he had heard the doctors give up all hope of his recovery? Did he recall how his friend, Bahá'u'lláh, had visited and cared for him? Did he remember his statements that Bahá'u'lláh had restored him to health? Did he reflect upon those prophetic words that he himself had once spoken to his own son about Bahá'u'lláh? "My son, those who now honor us with their lips would condemn and slander us if we failed for a moment to promote their interests. It is not that way with Bahá'u'lláh. Unlike other great men around us, he attracts a genuine love and devotion that neither time nor enemies can destroy."

Was the prime minister thinking of those hours of agonizing choice when Bahá'u'lláh had been a guest in his home, and he had delivered Him to the Black Pit in order to protect his position as chief minister of the land? Was he still hearing the sounds of the joyful chanting of those martyrs who had been slain in the most fiendish manner conceivable in the public square of Ṭihrán?

We shall never really know. We do know that the prime minister was deeply disturbed by Bahá'u'lláh when He came up out of that dungeon. He was shaken at the sight of what he had done to One from Whom he had received only kindnesses, on so many occasions. He could not remain antagonistic in that face-to-face encounter.

Mírzá Áqá Khán made yet another of his pitiful periodic efforts to atone for the past. "The warning you gave," he told Bahá'u'lláh, "has come true. What do you now advise me to do?"

Bahá'u'lláh replied that the prime minister should order the provincial governors to end the persecution of the innocent, to cease plundering their property and dishonoring their women. The government should abandon its feeling that it had the right to persecute the Báb's followers simply because of their religious beliefs.

This time, Mírzá Áqá Khán did not hesitate. On that same day he issued an order to the governors of the realm instructing them to cease all their actions against the followers of the Báb.

Náṣiri'd-Dín Sháh was not reconciled to Bahá'u'lláh's release from prison. He could no longer tolerate his victim's presence in Persia. Accordingly, he issued an immediate edict for the banishment of Bahá'u'lláh. Within ten days, on January 12, 1853, Bahá'u'lláh began the exile that was to take Him forever out of His homeland and lead Him at last to the side of Mount Carmel, the "Vineyard of God," in Israel.

Stripped of all His possessions, Bahá'u'lláh was given inadequate provisions and clothing for the cold wintry journey over the snowbound mountains of western Persia into Iraq.

The king and clergy were satisfied. At least they were rid of a hated enemy. The wings of death hovered about Bahá'u'lláh's Faith. To every eye, both the Báb and Bahá'u'lláh had been defeated. The redeemer of men, the unifier of the world, Bahá'u'lláh, appeared to be a colossal failure.

Náṣiri'd-Dín Sháh was confident that he had wiped out the new Faith. In fact, the opposite proved true. By sending Bahá'u'lláh into exile, Náṣiri'd-Dín Sháh made certain that the bright light of history would be shed upon every event associated with Bahá'u'lláh's exile. Future historians would study every word and action concerning that historic journey.

By banishing Bahá'u'lláh to Iraq, once the ancient land of Babylon, the shah drove his Prisoner by enforced exile to the historic site near where Ezekiel had seen his "vision" of the "Glory of God" by the ancient river Chebar.[5]

By his edict, Náṣiri'd-Din Sháh assured that Bahá'u'lláh would be exiled to the very spot where Ezekiel had made his prophecy concerning the One Who would come to the Holy Land from "the East," by way of "the gate."[6]

Bahá'u'lláh was on His way!

———— ❧ ————

9 ⚘ THE FIFTH KINGDOM FALLS

His hand is stretched out, and who shall turn it back?

Assassin! Assassin!

The hour had now come for the king of Persia himself to experience the retribution that his actions had entailed. Náṣiri'd-Dín Sháh was soon to be made, as promised by Bahá'u'lláh, "an object-lesson for the world."[1]

It happened on the occasion of the great jubilee celebration organized by the shah to honor his own station. The king looked forward to this occasion as his most glorious hour. He had elaborately planned to inaugurate a new era, one that he hoped would perpetuate his name in history.

The shah was greatly impressed by European civilization. Unlike his predecessors, he had visited France and other Western nations and sought to be remembered as the ruler who modernized Persia.

History had other plans.

Náṣiri'd-Dín Sháh went into the shrine of 'Abdu'l-'Azím, a venerated shah and a holy figure of Islam, to offer prayers on the eve of this historic occasion. Tomorrow, he told himself, he would campaign to woo back the affections of his subjects.

Bonfires lighted the night skies. Banners proclaimed the titles of the king. Trumpets and cymbals and drums declared on all sides the might and majesty of Náṣiri'd-Dín Sháh, the king of Persia.

Suddenly and without warning, the hand of the assassin struck. The royal sovereign fell dead on the pavement of the shrine. His ministers and companions were thrown into a panic, paralyzed by what had happened.

In order to delay the news of the shah's slaying, they carried his body from the shrine, and propped it up in the royal carriage. The dead king was supported by the prime minister himself as the carriage rolled through the streets.

The banners waved, the band struck up the music, the intimidated crowd shouted aloud its empty praise of a king it neither loved nor respected. The great jubilee festival was underway. It proclaimed a king who had become a propped-up corpse.

The shah's terror-stricken ministers, not knowing who might be next, passed along the dreaded words that were to become the signature of our modern political age: "Assassin! Assassin!"

The assassination of Náṣiri'd-Dín S̲h̲áh was at first blamed on the followers of the Báb. Like the Christians in ancient Rome or the Jews under Nazism, whenever any difficulty arose anywhere in the kingdom, the Bábís, and later the Bahá'ís, were the primary suspects, targets, and victims. The actual assassin was a certain Mírzá Riḍá, a follower of the notorious revolutionary Siyyid Jamálu'd-Dín-i-Afg̲h̲ání, who was a bitter and outspoken enemy of the Bahá'í Faith.

The fiendish minds, which had slain more than twenty thousand of the followers of this Faith, could not believe that their victims did not spend their days and nights in hatred, plotting revenge against their slayers. It was what they themselves would do, why not the Bahá'ís?

How little they knew of Bahá'u'lláh's teachings. He had denounced violence and had forbade the taking of life—"It is better to be killed than kill."[2] His teachings threw the integrity of His followers into sharp contrast with the cruelty and prejudice of Persia's rulers. Shortly before Náṣiri'd-Dín S̲h̲áh's death, a renowned teacher and poet called Varqá had been seized, along with his twelve-year-old son, Rúḥu'lláh.

The two Bábís were held together in the prison of Ṭihrán.

A brutal officer, the Ḥájibu'd-Dawlih, forced the son to stand and watch as he thrust a sword into the stomach of the boy's father. Unable to make Varqá plead for mercy, the enraged officer began to hack the father to pieces before the eyes of his son. Then he turned to Rúḥu'lláh.

"Now will you recant your faith?" he asked.

The boy's refusal was firm: "Never! Never!"

Frustrated with anger, the Ḥájibu'd-Dawlih seized a rope and strangled the child.

It is not surprising that Bahá'u'lláh included the people of Persia, who had so ruthlessly persecuted His Faith in His declaration that no one could dim God's shining light in the hearts of men once it had been ignited. He said, "Give heed to My warning, ye people of Persia! . . . He [God] shall perfect His light, albeit ye abhor it in the secret of your hearts."[3]

The House of the Qájár dynasty began to collapse about its kings. All the efforts to buttress it and prevent its downfall ended in failure.

The words of Isaiah the prophet seemed to echo from past centuries: "The Lord hath broken the staff of the wicked and the scepter of the rulers. . . . For the Lord of hosts hath purposed, and who shall disannul it? and his hand is stretched out, and who shall turn it back?"[4]

The dynasty of Náṣiri'd-Dín Sháh was rapidly approaching extinction. The walls were caving in on all sides. Soon every last one of its mighty kings and princes would be buried beneath the avalanche.

———— ❦ ————

This is the hour that no one can hold back!

Prince of Oppressors

In one of His warnings, Bahá'u'lláh foreshadowed the fate that overtook the Persian dynasty: "Ye shall, erelong, discover the consequences of that which ye shall have done in this vain life, and shall be repaid for them. . . . This is the day that shall inevitably come upon you, the hour that none can put back."[5]

The rulers of the Qájár dynasty, more than any other kings, were responsible for trying to crush the Revelation of God. From the hour of its birth until their own downfall, the Qájár rulers never once softened their implacable hostility.

Bahá'u'lláh did all in His power to awaken these rulers to their opportunity as emblems of justice, not of hatred: "If the rulers and kings of the earth, the symbols of the power of God, exalted be His glory, arise and resolve to dedicate themselves to whatever will promote the highest interests of the whole of humanity, the reign of justice will assuredly be established amongst the children of men, and the effulgence of its light will envelop the whole earth."[6]

Bahá'u'lláh had placed a grave responsibility upon the shoulders of Násiri'd-Dín Sháh personally, describing the shah as a "Prince of Oppressors." Násiri'd-Dín Sháh had been personally responsible for the martyrdom of the Báb. He was equally responsible for the banishments and lifelong persecutions of Bahá'u'lláh. Finally, he had given approval to the unjust slaying over a long period of time of thousands of innocent followers of the new Revelation.

Once again the Bible provides fascinating echoes of the events surrounding the story of Bahá'u'lláh. Is Náṣiri'd-Dín Sháh the "king of fierce countenance" who Daniel said would appear "in the latter time," the "king" who would "destroy" the "holy people?"

Was he the king who Daniel said would "stand" against the "Prince of princes" of the Lord? Was this the "king" who would be "broken" by this Redeemer of men Who, in a "time of trouble" such as the world has never seen, would "stand up" and deliver the "children" of God?[7]

One thing is certain, the day in which the king of Persia would be "broken" at last arrived.

------------ ❦ ------------

Wait thou, therefore, for
what hath been promised.

The Fifth Kingdom Falls

Bahá'u'lláh wrote to one of the ministers of Náṣiri'd-Dín Sháh a message that applied to the throne, the court, and the people of Persia. Although He had wished for them prosperity, security, and an everlasting sovereignty, they had rejected this heritage: "Erelong shall your days pass away, as shall pass away the days of those who now, with flagrant pride, vaunt themselves over their neighbor. Soon shall ye be gathered together in the presence of God, and shall be asked of your doings, and shall be repaid for what your hands have wrought, and wretched the abode of the wicked doers!"[8]

To any sincere individual, Bahá'u'lláh said that such deeds could only bring remorse: "By God! Wert thou to realize what thou hast done, thou wouldst surely weep sore over thyself, and wouldst flee for refuge to God."[9]

When all His entreaties and admonitions were disregarded, Bahá'u'lláh wrote these ominous words: "Wait thou, therefore, for what hath been promised . . . for this is a promise from Him Who is the Almighty, the All-Wise—a promise that will not prove untrue."[10]

Náṣiri'd-Dín Sháh's assassination was the first sign of the revolution that was to depose his successors and extinguish the Qájár dynasty.

Muẓaffari'd-Dín Sháh, the successor to Náṣiri'd-Din Sháh, was a weak and timid creature who was forced to sign the constitution that limited the royal powers. His successor, Muḥammad-'Alí Sháh, precipitated a revolution that led to his deposition.

Finally, Aḥmad Sháh, "a mere cipher and careless of his duties,"[11] ascended the throne. Anarchy increased, and the nation's financial condition, which had long been deplorable, now approached bankruptcy. The king had practically abandoned the country. He preferred the life of the European capitals to the stern duties of kingship. While the shah was abroad on one of his visits, parliament deposed him and proclaimed the extinction of the Qájár dynasty.

The House of Qájár had occupied the throne of Persia for 130 years.

The document that ended the dynasty was signed in 1925. This final humiliation took place in the government buildings that stand but a stone's throw from the site of that underground prison into which Náṣiri'd-Dín Sháh had cast Bahá'-

u'lláh. From that prison the sound of the voices of Bahá'u'lláh and His fellow prisoners had been heard by Náṣiri'd-Dín Sháh, the "Prince of Oppressors." Their song rang out in the hours of dawn and disturbed the shah as they chanted their prayers in praise of God, assured of that future victory: "In Him let the trusting trust!"

Bahá'u'lláh had kept His promise. The fifth kingdom had fallen.

10 ❦ 'AKKÁ

Great is the Cause, and great the Announcement!

The Announcement

Bahá'u'lláh's exile to Iraq in the Ottoman Turkish Empire did not leave Náṣiri'd-Dín Sháh or the Persian clergy in peace. Iraq contained a number of Muslim shrines that Persians were accustomed to visiting. The Persian clergy became concerned that the little party of exiles would begin to attract large numbers of these pilgrims to the new Cause.

The shah's government therefore began to bring pressure to bear on the sultan's ministers to move the Prisoner further away from the Persian borders. The Turkish and Persian empires had been antagonistic to one another, and the persecution of the exiles was one of the few points on which these two tyrannies agreed.

Accordingly, on April 22, 1863, Bahá'u'lláh was advised that He was to leave at once and move with His companions to the imperial capital, Constantinople.

Before this enforced departure, Bahá'u'lláh made the first formal declaration of His mission. The day of "one fold and one Shepherd" had arrived,[1] He said, and He was the one awaited by the followers of all the world's religions.

This historic announcement took place in a garden outside the city of Baghdad. It was made during the twelve days between April 21 and May 2, 1863, and is celebrated by Bahá'ís today in every part of the world as the holiest and most joyful event in the entire Bahá'í calendar. It is called the Festival of Riḍván (Arabic for "paradise").

Visitors flowed constantly from Baghdad to that famous garden so that all might make their last farewell to the Visitor Whom they had come to love dearly. It was hard to believe that these were the people who such a short time before had readily believed the slander spread about the exiles by agents of Náṣiri'd-Dín Sháh.

A large concourse of people, men, women, and children, thronged the approaches to Bahá'u'lláh's house in Baghdad on the day of His departure for the Garden of Riḍván outside the city. They came from all directions for one last glimpse of Him. City officials, clergymen, merchants and notables, as well as the poor and the orphaned, the beggars and the outcasts, all watched Bahá'u'lláh depart out of their city amidst weeping and lamentation.

The huge crowds that surrounded Bahá'u'lláh on the day of His departure from the Garden of Riḍván were even more impressive. Mounted on a red roan stallion which His loved ones had purchased for His journey, Bahá'u'lláh rode through the weeping crowds. They pressed in on Him from all sides. Clothed in majesty and surrounded by love, Bahá'u'lláh began the first stage of His historic exile to Constantinople.

Bahá'u'lláh left forever the valley of the Tigris and Euphrates rivers, the spot where Ezekiel had seen the "Glory of God" in his vision. Bahá'u'lláh was now beginning His circuitous route westward to Israel.

His fame as a saint and teacher preceded Him. The same tokens of respect and devotion that were showered upon Bahá'u'lláh in Baghdad now followed Him all along the route of His travels northward. The journey to the port city of

Sámsún on the Black Sea took 110 days. As Bahá'u'lláh passed through the villages en route, a welcoming delegation would be waiting. They would rush out to meet Him immediately before His arrival, while another delegation would accompany Him for some distance as He departed out of their village.

Bahá'u'lláh and His companions came at last to the Black Sea. Sighting the shores of the sea from His caravan, Bahá'u'lláh wrote a moving Tablet alluding to the "grievous and tormenting" sorrows that still awaited Him.[2]

The group was put on board a Turkish steamer on which they crossed the Black Sea, and three days later they disembarked at the famous port of Constantinople. The great capital city of Turkey had once been called the "Dome of Islam." Because of the injustices and cruelty of Sulṭán 'Abdu'l-'Azíz, it was to be described by Bahá'u'lláh as "the throne of tyranny."[3] Bahá'u'lláh knew that His brief hours of joy and rest were at an end and that His torments were to begin again: two further banishments were still to come, and renewed attempts would be made on His life. All of these attempted assassinations would be unsuccessful.

Bahá'u'lláh, in the years ahead, would arrive at last in Israel and would walk on the side of the "Mountain of God." He was traveling to the Holy Land, as promised by Isaiah, "by way of the sea." In one single chapter of praise for the Promised One of the last days, Isaiah declares that this "chosen" Servant of the "seed of Abraham" was that "righteous man from the east" Whom God had raised up to "rule over kings" and Who would "pass safely" to His destination, Israel, "even by the way that he had not gone by his feet."[4] The Old Testament prophet Micah had also foreseen the journey "from sea to sea" on the way from the East to the Holy Land, where He would redeem mankind.[5]

But who was there to read and understand and come to His aid?

The Grand Vizir turned the color of a corpse.

The Throne of Tyranny

After the long and taxing journey to Constantinople, Bahá'-u'lláh was permitted to remain in the capital less than four months. The sultan of Turkey could not tolerate in the capital city the kind of honor that had been paid to Bahá'u'lláh along the route of His journey from Baghdad. Only the person of the king was considered a suitable object for such attention.

Bahá'u'lláh was summarily banished once again. This sudden and cruel further banishment represented "a virtual coalition between the Turkish and Persian imperial governments" against one man and His tiny band of companions, their wives and children—less than eighty persons in all. This time, Bahá'u'lláh did not accept the edict meekly. He replied with a forceful letter of His own.

On that very same day, Bahá'u'lláh sent His reply by special messenger of 'Alí Páshá, the prime minister of the sultan. This special messenger, Shamsí Big, delivered the letter personally into the hands of 'Alí Páshá. He has left the following eyewitness account of that meeting:

"I know not what that letter contained for no sooner had the Grand Vizír 'Alí Páshá perused it that he turned the color of a corpse, and said: 'It is as if the King of Kings were issuing his behest to his humblest vassal king and regulating his conduct."

<u>Sh</u>amsí Big added, "So grievous was the condition that I backed out of his presence."[6]

The order for Bahá'u'lláh's departure was executed at once. Bahá'u'lláh, His family and His companions unprepared, began their third successive banishment. Some rode in wagons, some on pack animals. Others sat silently among their few remaining possessions, atop of carts pulled by oxen.

It was a bitter cold December morning when the Turkish officers pushed them along their way. Bahá'u'lláh Himself declared that the cruelty and abasement that were heaped upon Himself and His companions during that exile were unnecessary and unpardonable. He has testified that none of those who accompanied Him had the necessary clothing "to protect them from the cold in that freezing winter."

Nabíl, who accompanied Bahá'u'lláh on the journey, recalled, "A cold of such intensity prevailed that year, that nonagenarians could not recall its like." Animals froze and perished in the snows. "To obtain water from the springs, a great fire had to be lighted in their immediate neighborhood, and kept burning for a couple of hours before they thawed out."[7]

It is not surprising therefore that Bahá'u'lláh addressed Sultán 'Abdu'l-'Azíz in strong language: "Hearken, O King, to the speech of Him that speaketh the truth. . . . Bring thyself to account ere thou art summoned to a reckoning. . . . Thou art God's shadow on earth. Strive, therefore, to act in such a manner as befitteth so eminent, so august a station. . . . Let thine ear be attentive, O King, to the words We have addressed to thee. Let the oppressor desist from His tyranny, and cut off the perpetrators of injustice from among them that profess thy faith. . . . Be not forgetful of the law of God in whatever thou desirest to achieve, now or in the days to come."[8]

On the eve of His departure from Constantinople, Bahá'-u'lláh wrote to the Persian ambassador, who had incited the Turkish authorities to bring about His banishment by alarming their fears of the exiles. Bahá'u'lláh recalled to the ambassador's mind the more than twenty thousand followers who had already given their lives for this Faith in Persia. He explained the futility of trying to stamp out the fire of the love of God in men's hearts by persecution: "What did it profit thee, and such as are like thee, to slay, year after year, so many of the oppressed, and to inflict upon them manifold afflictions, when they have increased a hundredfold. . . . [God's] Cause transcends any and every plan ye devise."[9]

Then Bahá'u'lláh made a promise that time and history would soon bring to fulfillment: "Know this much: Were all the governments on earth to unite and take My life and the lives of all who bear this Name [Bahá'í], this Divine Fire would never be quenched. His Cause will rather encompass all the kings of the earth, nay all that hath been created from water and clay. . . . Whatever may yet befall Us, great shall be our gain, and manifest the loss wherewith they shall be afflicted."[10]

Bahá'u'lláh and His companions traveled toward Adrianople through snow, rain, and storm. At times they were forced to make night marches, but at last they reached their destination. This was the furthest point in Bahá'u'lláh's repeated exiles. He called it the "remote prison."

Bahá'u'lláh was the first of the founders of the great re-vealed religions to touch upon European soil. This was yet another way in which Bahá'u'lláh's mission linked together both the East and the West. Bahá'u'lláh was the first of these Messengers of God to proclaim His Faith from the West as well as from the East.

Náṣiri'd-Dín Sháh had imprisoned Bahá'u'lláh in the Black Pit in Ṭihrán, His native city. There Bahá'u'lláh's ministry had begun. Bahá'u'lláh had been banished to another land to si-lence His tongue and weaken His influence. In the famed val-ley of the Tigris and Euphrates rivers, Bahá'u'lláh had for-mally declared the purpose of His mission to His companions and to the world. Alarmed at the Prisoner's growing prestige and power, Náṣiri'd-Dín Sháh had conspired with Sulṭán 'Abdu'l-'Azíz to banish Him to Constantinople, farther yet from the circle of His relatives, friends, and followers. The kings sent Him to another continent, Europe. There, in the midst of the "throne of tyranny" Bahá'u'lláh, in the capital city of Constantinople, launched the first stage of the public procla-mation of His mission to the world.

Now Bahá'u'lláh was banished yet again, this time to a remote outpost where it was felt He would be powerless to influence anyone of importance. He would be cut off from the world. There in Adrianople, contrary to the schemes of kings, Bahá'u'lláh's mission reached its high-point. He wrote His historic Tablet to the kings and rulers of the world. There He launched in its flood-tide the proclamation of His Faith to the world on a scale unprecedented in the religious history of mankind.

Every persecution, every suppression designed by the kings to render Bahá'u'lláh impotent, however devastating in the physical sufferings He sustained, was followed by a greater outpouring of teaching and spirit. Sufferings the kings devised for their Prisoner proved only to be preludes to a greater unfolding of God's purpose for mankind.

The greatest suffering, and the full unfolding, lay ahead.

He that sitteth in the heavens shall laugh.

The Final Banishment

For nearly five years Bahá'u'lláh was a prisoner and exile in the remote provincial city of Adrianople. During those turbulent years Bahá'u'lláh survived three more attempts on His life. His enemies twice tried to poison Him and conspired to have Him slain in the public bath. All were unsuccessful.

Bahá'u'lláh now turned to the task of revealing God's guidance for the governments as well as the peoples of the world. Some of His most important and extensive writings date from this period. Nabíl, the Bábí historian, writes, "A number of secretaries were busy day and night, and yet they were unable to cope with the task [of transcribing the Revelation]."[11]

Bahá'u'lláh during His lifetime wrote over one hundred volumes, which dealt with the various problems facing man and his society. One of the most fruitful periods of His entire mission was during His days in Adrianople. Bahá'u'lláh Himself affirms the copiousness of His writings during those months in Turkey, saying, "That which hath already been revealed in this land [Adrianople] secretaries are incapable of transcribing."[12]

On another occasion, Bahá'u'lláh declared, "In those days the equivalent of all that hath been sent down aforetime unto the Prophets hath been revealed."[13]

These writings were part of the historic worldwide proclamation of His Faith to the kings and rulers of the earth. This proclamation had its first beginnings in Constantinople, when Bahá'u'lláh sent His powerful letter to the prime minister of Sultán 'Abdu'l-'Azíz following the king's decree banishing Him to Adrianople. This proclamation reached its zenith in Adrianople.

There Bahá'u'lláh wrote His most momentous letter to the crowned heads of the world. For "the first time He directed His words collectively to the entire company of the monarchs of East and West."[14] Bahá'u'lláh warned these rulers that "divine chastisement" would "assail" them "from every direction" if they failed in their responsibility to consider the new social and spiritual principles that God was revealing for a united world. Bahá'u'lláh prophesied the triumph of this Cause even if "no king be found who would turn his face towards [God]."

Those who took the time to listen to His words and grasp the significance of His teachings were deeply moved. The essence of His message to the kings and rulers of the world, and to the peoples of the earth, can be found in those writings that streamed constantly from His pen during those years in Adrianople.

Social justice was the basis of almost every instruction that Bahá'u'lláh issued to the leaders of men. He constantly urged those in authority to shield and shelter the needy ones. He encouraged them to protect the rights of the underprivileged and to uplift and instill hope in the downtrodden. In Bahá'-u'lláh's own words: "O Ye Rich Ones on Earth! The poor in your midst are My trust; guard ye My trust, and be not intent only on your own ease."[15]

And in another place, "Tell the rich of the midnight sighing of the poor. . . . to be poor in all save God is a wondrous gift, belittle not the value thereof; for in the end it will make thee rich in God."[16]

This "most glorious phase" in Bahá'u'lláh's mission is filled with His counsels for the protection of the peoples of the world. It will forever remain as the "zenith" of His ministry on earth. Bahá'u'lláh urged all the leaders of the world to unite in a program that would forever end the unjust extremes of wealth and poverty. This was more than a hundred years ago! He wrote, "O ye rulers of the earth! . . . Hearken unto the counsel given you . . . that haply both ye and the poor may attain unto tranquillity and peace. We beseech God to assist the kings of the earth to establish peace on earth."[17]

During these fateful days in Adrianople, Bahá'u'lláh "arose with matchless power" to proclaim the mission "with which He had been entrusted."[18] He broadcast it to the rulers of men in both the East and the West, those leaders who held the reins of temporal power in their grasp.

Bahá'u'lláh was Himself "bent with sorrow" and still suffering from the effects of the last attempt on His life. He was well aware that a further banishment was impending. In spite of all these obstacles and perils, the Faith of Bahá'u'lláh during this period began to shine "in its meridian glory" and to demonstrate the power with which it was invested.[19]

The Turkish government now yielded entirely to the pressure of the Persian ambassador and decided to send the exiles to a place that would both isolate them and assure their early deaths. A decree was issued commanding Bahá'u'lláh's fourth banishment to the dreaded penal colony of 'Akká.

The companions of Bahá'u'lláh were seized by the authorities in their homes and on the streets of Adrianople in a surprise arrest. They were questioned, deprived of their papers, and flung into prison. Several times members of the group were summoned before the authorities and questioned concerning the exact number of Bahá'u'lláh's family and friends. Rumors ran through the village that "they were to be dispersed to different places or secretly put to death."[20]

Sulṭán 'Abdu'l-'Azíz had been assured by his ministers that neither Bahá'u'lláh nor His Faith could survive in the pestilential atmosphere of 'Akká. This fortress-city was the most dreaded prison in all the Turkish empire. The sultan's advisors felt confident that Bahá'u'lláh would soon perish in that vile place. In fact, they were taking part in a spiritual drama that the prophets of the past had foreseen and described.

By banishing Bahá'u'lláh to 'Akká, these enemies believed that they were carrying out the orders of their ruler, Sulṭán 'Abdu'l-'Azíz. In reality, they were instruments for the fulfillment of promises made by God in sacred scripture long before.

Although Bahá'u'lláh's companions, until almost the last moment of their departure from Turkey, were uncertain where He would be sent, Bahá'u'lláh Himself, the "Ancient Beauty," the object of so many wonderful and thrilling prophecies in the holy books of the past, was only too aware of His ultimate destination. He knew where He would ultimately be banished years before the event. As far back as the first years of His banishment to Adrianople, Bahá'u'lláh had already alluded to His future arrival at the fortress-city of 'Akká.

Bahá'u'lláh wrote about the worldwide triumph of His Faith that would follow that historic arrival. During those earliest years in Turkey, Bahá'u'lláh also hinted at the importance and significance of that future historic landing at 'Akká. His words were, in reality, a prophecy. He wrote, "Upon Our arrival, We were welcomed with banners of light, whereupon the Voice of the Spirit cried out saying, 'Soon will all that dwell on earth be enlisted under these banners.'"[21]

———— ❧ ————

Tell the king that this territory
will pass out of his hands.

The Journey by Sea

On August 12, 1868, Bahá'u'lláh and His family began their four-day journey to Gallipoli, the first stage of their final banishment. They were escorted by a Turkish captain and a detachment of soldiers. The party stopped en route at several towns.

At Káshánih, Bahá'u'lláh began one of His most famous letters to the kings of the earth. It was completed a short time later, at Gyawur-Kyuy. Before leaving Turkey, Bahá'u'lláh made it clear that He would never forget that land. He asserted that He had "deposited beneath every tree and every stone a trust, which God will erelong bring forth through the power of truth."[22]

The significance of these words was soon to become apparent.

Bahá'u'lláh and His companions finally reached Gallipoli, where they spent three nights. This was to be their last stop in Turkey.

Even at that late hour, Bahá'u'lláh gave 'Abdu'l-'Azíz one final opportunity to repent of his past actions. Bahá'u'lláh sent a verbal message to the king through a Turkish officer named 'Umar.

Bahá'u'lláh requested that Sulṭán 'Abdu'l-'Azíz grant Him a ten-minute interview during which the king could make any test he wished, so that he might determine for himself the truth or falsehood of Bahá'u'lláh's Faith. The request was not granted.

Not one of Bahá'u'lláh's attempts at such a confrontation with the kings, their ministers, or the clergy had ever been accepted.

Bahá'u'lláh prepared to depart for 'Akká, a city that had once been part of the ancient land of Canaan. According to sacred scripture, Canaan was the land that would be inherited in the last days by one of the "seed" of Abraham.

Bahá'u'lláh was descended from Abraham through His third wife, Katurah. How tender and beautiful is this story of Abraham and His seed, Bahá'u'lláh. How closely Their missions were bound together. How remarkably Their stories parallel each other.

In the valley of the Tigris and Euphrates rivers, Abraham proclaimed the oneness of God. In that same valley, Bahá'u'lláh proclaimed the oneness of all religions, races, and nations. Abraham was exiled from that valley to the land of Canaan.

Bahá'u'lláh followed the same exile to that same land, where He completed His teachings and laws for the salvation of all humanity.

In a Tablet revealed on the eve of His banishment to the penal colony of 'Akká, Bahá'u'lláh declared, "Had Abraham attained it [this day], He too, falling prostrate on the ground . . . would have cried: 'Mine heart is filled with peace, O Thou Lord of all that is in heaven and on earth! I testify that Thou hast unveiled before mine eyes all the glory of Thy power and the full majesty of Thy law!'"[23]

The hour had come at last for Bahá'u'lláh to leave European soil and begin His journey to the Holy Land. When Ḥasan Effendi, the officer who had escorted Him from Adrianople, was taking his leave of Bahá'u'lláh, the Turkish captain was given yet another message for the sultan: "Tell the king that this territory will pass out of his hands, and that his affairs will be thrown into confusion."[24]

Bahá'u'lláh wanted Sulṭán 'Abdu'l-'Azíz to know that on this occasion, He was speaking not as a prisoner and an exile, but as a Messenger of God. He was addressing the king with the same authority with which Moses, Christ, and Muḥammad had spoken of old. One of His followers, Áqá Riḍá, recorded that scene for posterity: "To this [statement] Bahá'u'lláh furthermore added: 'Not I speak these words, but God speaketh them.' In those moments He was uttering verses which we, who were downstairs, could overhear. They were spoken with such vehemence and power that, methinks, the foundations of the house itself trembled."[25]

Bahá'u'lláh embarked for 'Akká via Egypt. The Persian ambassador promptly informed the Persian consul in Egypt that the Turkish government had withdrawn its protection over the followers of Bahá'u'lláh. "You are now free to treat them as you please," was the essence of this information forwarded by that persistent enemy.

The threats and trials that faced Bahá'u'lláh as He headed toward His final exile were so grievous that He warned His companions about the dangers and hardships that lay ahead.

Bahá'u'lláh urged those who did not feel stout-hearted enough to face the sufferings yet to come to feel free to leave for any destination that they might desire. Those who chose to accompany Him, Bahá'u'lláh said, would find it impossible to leave in the future. Bahá'u'lláh warned them that "this journey will be unlike any of the previous journeys."[26]

If a bird flies over 'Akká, it dies!

The King of Glory Enters the Gate

On August 21, 1868, Bahá'u'lláh and His companions were taken on board an Austrian-Lloyd steamer bound for the Holy Land. The ship touched first at Modelli and Smyrna. At Alexandria, Bahá'u'lláh was transferred to another ship that stopped at Port Said and Jaffa.

On August 31, the vessel arrived at the port of Haifa. It anchored at sea below the foot of Mount Carmel, the "Nest of the Prophets" and the "Vineyard of God."

The "Glory of God" had come home at last!

He had come "by way of the sea," as promised in sacred scripture. He had crossed the Black Sea, and now the Mediterranean Sea to arrive in a land "sanctified by the Revelation of Moses, honored by the lives and labors of the Hebrew patriarchs, judges, kings, and prophets." It was revered "as the cradle of Christianity"; honored as the place where Zoroaster conversed "with some of the prophets of Israel"; a land associated with the "night journey" of the Apostle of Islam, Muḥammad; a land linked with the Founders of Judaism, Christianity, Zoroastrianism, Islam, and now with both the Herald and Founder of the Baháʼí Faith, the Báb and Baháʼuʼlláh, Whose remains are entombed there.[27]

David not only described ʻAkká as the Strong City in his Psalms, he also predicted that the "king of Glory" would come through the "gates" and "not keep silence."

And at last He had come!

Hosea had described ʻAkká as "a door of hope." Isaiah foretold that ʻAkká would be a refuge for the "herds" of God to lie down in with safety in the last days.

By the action of His enemies, Baháʼuʼlláh, the exile of Baghdad, of Constantinople, and Adrianople, was to spend the last third of His entire life, and over half of the duration of His earthly mission in that sacred land.

Baháʼuʼlláh's son ʻAbduʼl-Bahá was also a prisoner on that historic occasion. He wrote of Baháʼuʼlláh's arrival in that land: "It is difficult to understand how Baháʼuʼlláh could have been obliged to leave Persia, and to pitch His tent in this Holy Land, but for the persecution of His enemies, His banishment and exile."[28]

The shah of Persia and the sultan of Turkey, the two supreme temporal rulers of the destinies of both Sunni and Shia Islam, had imprisoned Baháʼuʼlláh in what they considered the ultimate prison. They had shut Him up in a city so forlorn that it was described as "the metropolis of the owl." So unsanitary and foul was the atmosphere of the fortress-city with its prevalence of malaria, typhoid, and dysentery that it was said in a proverb, "If a bird flies over 'Akká, it dies!"

In retrospect, these attempts on the part of the kings to destroy Bahá'u'lláh seem merely pathetic. The scriptures of the major religions make clear why every one of these efforts ended in disaster. In spite of the repeated and combined efforts of kings and clergy to prevent it, the Glory of God appeared at last on the side of God's holy mountain, Carmel.

These rulers of the world were foiled at every step. They added immeasurably to Bahá'u'lláh's cup of sorrow, but they were powerless to prevent Him from fulfilling His destiny. That had been foretold. Every step along the way, Bahá'u'lláh fulfilled prophecy after prophecy from the holy books of those kings until, in spite of them, He came at last to God's "holy hill."

This story itself, this tragedy of blind kings, had been clearly foreshadowed in the book of Psalms. The prophecy declared:

The kings of the earth set themselves, and the rulers take counsel together, against the Lord. . . . He that sitteth in the heavens shall laugh: the Lord shall have them in derision. Then shall He speak unto them in His wrath. . . . Yet have I set my king upon my holy hill of Zion. . . . thou shalt dash them in pieces like a potter's vessel. Be wise now therefore, O ye kings: be instructed, ye judges of the earth. . . . Blessed are all they that put their trust in Him.[29]

The king of Turkey had failed to put his trust in Bahá'u'lláh. No matter how often that assistance had been offered to him, the king had rejected it. The judges, ministers, and leaders of that land, following the lead of their sovereign, were not wise in their judgments. Their downfall and disappearance from living history was even then being fashioned by the Hand of God.

All of them shall be slain except one,
who shall reach the plain of 'Akká.

The Banquet-Hall of God

The arrival of Bahá'u'lláh in 'Akká began the final phase of His forty-year long ministry, a period of time itself repeatedly emphasized in sacred scripture. Bahá'u'lláh had come to the heart of Judaism and Christianity. Already His exile had taken Him to the "strongholds" of Islam.

It is hard to understand the ignorance of these rulers of Islam, Sulṭán 'Abdu'l-'Azíz and Náṣiri'd-Dín Sháh, concerning the references so prevalent throughout their own sacred writings, to all these events. Unlike the kings of Christendom, these rulers of Islam, as many of their titles indicated, were an integral part of the religious system. Yet they were oblivious of the traditional prophecies recorded in their own holy books—prophecies that they had brought to a staggering fulfillment by their own cruel acts against Bahá'u'lláh. Their attitude speaks volumes about the sincerity of their belief in their own faith. For example:

Muḥammad, the Prophet of Islam, had referred glowingly to this very prison-city of 'Akká. He called it "A city to which God hath shown His special mercy." And in another place He described it as a city "by the shore of the sea whose whiteness is pleasing unto God."[30]

From the traditional prophecies so highly honored in the sacred writings of both Turkey and Persia could be found these further astonishing words that 'Abdu'l-'Azíz and Náṣiri'd-Dín Sháh might have done well to ponder:

"Blessed the man that hath visited 'Akká, and blessed he that hath visited the visitor of 'Akká."

"He that raiseth therein the call to prayer, his voice will be lifted up unto Paradise."

"The poor of 'Akká are the kings of Paradise and the princes thereof."

"A month in 'Akká is better than a thousand years elsewhere."[31]

Why? No one really understood the mystery until Bahá'-u'lláh's arrival.

And finally, one of the most remarkable prophecies of all. It is especially significant when one studies the history of the martyrdom of the Herald of Bahá'u'lláh's Faith, the Báb. Some twenty thousand of His followers were slain—a fate that Bahá'u'lláh Himself escaped time after time in Persia, Iraq, and Turkey. He was the only intimate of the Báb to escape Persia. The prophecies spoke repeatedly of the One Who would appear in the year 1260 (AD 1844).[32] He would be the first of two such Messengers. One of these traditional prophecies foretells the martyrdom of this holy Messenger and many of His followers, and declares, "All of them shall be slain except One Who shall reach the plain of 'Akká, the Banquet-Hall of God."[33]

After reaching the "plain of 'Akká" Bahá'u'lláh had written to the kings of the world concerning that mighty banquet-of-God that He had offered to them for the nourishment and unity of mankind. Bahá'u'lláh said, "He Who is the Unconditioned is come. . . . that He may quicken all created things . . . and unify the world, and gather all men around this Table that hath been sent down from heaven."[34]

The arrival of Bahá'u'lláh in the Holy Land fulfilled as well the astonishing prophecies from the book of Micah. Micah, as had Isaiah and Daniel, foretold both the first and second coming in the glory of the Father, Bahá'u'lláh. The prophecies fulfilled by Bahá'u'lláh seem almost a road-map of spiritual life. They describe His journeys from Persia to Mount Carmel. These prophecies alone should be evidence enough for all humankind.

Micah prophesied that in the last days, when corruption and hatred have filled the earth, the Redeemer will come from Babylon to Israel. Bahá'u'lláh was exiled to Israel from Baghdad, near the site of ancient Babylon. Then in the course of one chapter Micah gives an amazing answer to those who ridiculed him, saying: "Where is the Lord thy God?"[35]

"In that day also, he shall come even to thee from Assyria." Bahá'u'lláh came from what was once in the midst of the Assyrian empire.

"In that day also he shall come even to thee . . . from the fortified cities." Bahá'u'lláh came from the fortified city of Constantinople to the fortified city of 'Akká.

"In that day also he shall come even to thee . . . from the fortress even to the river." Bahá'u'lláh came to the ancient river Belus from the fortress of 'Akká when He was released from prison.

"In that day also he shall come even to thee . . . from sea to sea." Bahá'u'lláh came across the Black Sea in exile to Constantinople, and across the Mediterranean Sea on His last exile to the Holy Land.

"In that day also he shall come even to thee . . . from mountain to mountain." Bahá'u'lláh came from a mountain in the valley of the Tigris and Euphrates rivers (from ancient Babylon) to Mount Carmel, in Israel.

In the next verse, Micah says the "land shall be desolate" when the Redeemer arrives. 'Akká was described as the "most desolate of cities" at this time. After Bahá'u'lláh's coming that arid, "desolate" area began slowly to "blossom as the rose."

In the following verse, Micah says that this "Lord of Salvation" will "feed" his flock "in the midst of Carmel." Bahá'u'lláh announced on the side of Mount Carmel that all the prophecies had been fulfilled. The World Center of His Faith has its headquarters "in the midst of Carmel," from where Bahá'u'lláh's teachings are now going out into all parts of the planet to "feed" the peoples and nations of the world.

In the next verse, Micah says that God will "shew unto him," the Redeemer, "marvellous things" for forty years. Bahá'u'lláh's mission lasted exactly forty years, during which time He shared with the kings and leaders of men the "wonderful things" He had been "shewn" by God.

Micah prophesied that in the last days the "house of the Lord" will be "established" in the mountain, many nations will "flow" unto it, and the "law" shall "go forth" and Israel shall become "a strong nation." In Bahá'u'lláh's own words, "These passages stand in need of no commentary."[36] Their truth is self-evident.

Is there anywhere in history a more remarkable story? One would expect the banners to be flying and the bands to be playing and the hearts of men singing with joy at the arrival of the Promised One of all Ages on the side of God's holy mountain. What really happened?

Bahá'u'lláh has written about His arrival in that dreaded prison, saying, "None knoweth what befell Us, except God, the Almighty, the All-Knowing."[37]

So grave and critical were the first nine years of His imprisonment in that penal colony, that Bahá'u'lláh wrote, "Know thou, that upon Our arrival at this Spot, We chose to designate it as the 'Most Great Prison.' Though previously subjected in another land [Persia] to chains and fetters, We yet refused to call it by that name. . . . Ponder thereon, O ye endued with understanding!"[38]

But He assured His followers that "Though afflicted with countless tribulations, which We have suffered at the hands of Our enemies, We have proclaimed unto all the rulers of the earth what God hath willed to proclaim, that all nations may know that no manner of affliction can deter the Pen of the Ancient of Days from achieving its purpose. . . . The hosts of the earth can never dismay Thee, nor can the dominion of all peoples and nations deter Thee from executing Thy purpose."[39]

The decree exiling Bahá'u'lláh to 'Akká was dated July 26, 1868. The text was read publicly, soon after Bahá'u'lláh's arrival, in the principal mosques of the city, as a warning to the population.

The sultan feared that the people of 'Akká might fall under the seemingly magic charm of Bahá'u'lláh's spell as had the people in Baghdad and Adrianople. The king was determined that this time Bahá'u'lláh and His companions should be made objects of derision and hatred by the inhabitants of the city of 'Akká. The sultan resolved to make no mistake this time.

His decree condemned Bahá'u'lláh, His family, and His followers to perpetual banishment. It also "stipulated their strict incarceration and forbade them to associate either with each other or with the local inhabitants."[40] The townspeople of 'Akká were encouraged to persecute and humiliate Bahá'u'lláh, His family, and His friends in every way possible. These captives were described to the people as enemies of both God and man.

By these acts of hatred, the sultan set the final seal on the extinction of his own outward splendor. All these events led to the doom of imperial Turkey, the "throne of tyranny."

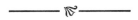

11 ⊸ THE SIXTH KINGDOM FALLS

Abandon not the interests of thy people.

A Warning

Sulṭán 'Abdu'l-'Azíz, head of the Turkish House of 'Uthmán, had conspired with the shah of Persia on three successive occasions against the Messenger of God, in Whose coming he claimed to believe. Every day the sultan, as caliph of Islam, read the Qur'án, in which the divine promise was made.

Whenever information concerning Bahá'u'lláh and His companions reached the ministers of the sultan, it was immediately distorted and twisted into false accusations against Him. Bahá'u'lláh and His fellow-exiles were represented to the king as "a mischief to the world" and as "deserving of every chastisement and punishment."[1]

Bahá'u'lláh wrote to Sulṭán 'Abdu'l-'Azíz, warning him against such deceit on the part of his advisors: "Beware, O King, that thou gather not around thee such ministers as follow the desires of a corrupt inclination . . . and manifestly betrayed their trust."[2]

Bahá'u'lláh was concerned more with the effect that such unjust ministers would have upon the welfare of the king's subjects rather than upon Himself. Bahá'u'lláh wrote, "Abandon not the interests of thy people to the mercy of such ministers as these. . . . He that acteth treacherously towards God will, also, act treacherously towards his king. Nothing whatever can deter such a man from evil, nothing can hinder him from betraying his neighbor, nothing can induce him to walk uprightly."[3]

He understood only too well the graft with which the sultanic empire was riddled and knew how gravely the poor people suffered at the hands of these greedy and corrupt ministers of state. Bahá'u'lláh strongly emphasized this grave danger in His letter to Sulṭán 'Abdu'l-'Azíz, saying, "Take heed that thou resign not the reins of the affairs of thy state into the hands of others, and repose not thy confidence in ministers unworthy of thy trust. . . . Beware that thou allow not the wolf to become the shepherd of God's flock, and surrender not the fate of His loved ones to the mercy of the malicious . . . , and walk not in the paths of the oppressor."[4]

Bahá'u'lláh counseled the king to be personally responsible for the welfare of his people. He warned the sultan not to permit others to seize his power and to use it unjustly by persecuting those beneath them. "Seize thou, and hold firmly within the grasp of thy might, the reins of the affairs of thy people, and examine in person whatever pertaineth unto them. Let nothing escape thee, for therein lieth the highest good. . . . Thou canst best praise Him [God] if thou lovest His loved ones, and dost safeguard and protect His servants from the mischief of the treacherous, that none may any longer oppress them."[5]

These warnings went unheeded. 'Abdu'l-'Azíz, enormously self-indulgent, surrendered all practical concerns into the hands of some of the most ambitious and amoral politicians in his domains. They could assure him stability and prosperity, he felt.

In fact their greed and injustice were to pull the sultan and his throne down when they themselves fell.

"Leave it to God and history to judge between us."

The Strong City

The tempo of Bahá'u'lláh's call to the rulers of the world was greatly increased and intensified during these "days of stress." The greater His sufferings, the more forceful was Bahá'u'lláh's call to the world to arise and eliminate all prejudice and injustice.

He wrote, "O kings of the earth! We see you increasing every year your expenditures, and laying the burden thereof on your subjects. This, verily, is wholly and grossly unjust. Fear the sighs and tears of this Wronged One, and lay not excessive burdens on your peoples."[6]

And, in one of His most moving denunciations of such tyrant kings as Sulṭán 'Abdu'l-'Azíz of Turkey, Bahá'u'lláh wrote, "Do not rob them [your people] to rear palaces for yourselves; nay rather choose for them that which ye choose for yourselves. Thus We unfold to your eyes that which profiteth you, if ye but perceive."[7]

He urged the leaders of men to look upon their subjects as their most important and valued asset. He said, "Your people are your treasures. Beware lest your rule violate the commandments of God, and ye deliver your wards to the hands of the robber. By them ye rule, by their means ye subsist, by their aid ye conquer. Yet, how disdainfully ye look upon them! How strange, how very strange!"[8]

Bahá'u'lláh's strong defense of the rights of the poor and downtrodden against the mighty rulers of earth was yet another of those remarkable events that had been foreseen so long ago in sacred scripture. The Old Testament had prophesied, "O give thanks unto the Lord. . . . To him which smote great kings . . . Who remembered us in our low estate . . . And hath redeemed us from our enemies."⁹

Bahá'u'lláh had done just that. The time for the redemption of all the peoples of the earth from such enemies had arrived. The hour for the "smiting" of great kings had come.

Sul⎯t⎯án 'Abdu'l-'Azíz ignored Bahá'u'lláh's counsels. In spite of all His warnings, the sultan permitted his ministers to continue their persecution of the Prisoner and His companions. Bahá'u'lláh then forecast the inevitable retribution that would soon overtake the king, reminding the sultan in these words, "Ye failed utterly to take heed . . . ye waxed more heedless. . . . Be expectant, however, for the wrath of God is ready to overtake you. Erelong will ye behold that which hath been sent down from the Pen of My command."¹⁰

Bahá'u'lláh's words to the leaders of humanity made it unmistakably clear that this grave worldwide struggle, in which entire kingdoms were involved, was not a conflict between Himself and those who were in authority. It was a planetary clash between those who loved the things of God and those who loved the things of men. It was an inevitable battle between physical and moral forces. It was a struggle between the material and the spiritual; between age-old inequities on the one hand and true justice on the other.

All the tragedies now engulfing the world had come about because humankind had turned away from God and was drowning in purely materialistic concerns. Humanity's animal nature was in ascendancy, and until people turned to God, they would continue to suffer greater tragedies and more violent calamities. For this reason, Bahá'u'lláh called upon the kings to assist Him in rescuing humanity from this threatening disaster. He could only point the way and give the guidance. The leadership must come from the temporal rulers.

He challenged the sultan, his ministers, and his priests to examine the Bahá'í teachings with an open mind. He made it plain that if this Faith was true, there was no king who could prevent its rising. No man can hold back the sun of a new day.

Bahá'u'lláh also pointed out that if this Faith was *not* the truth, then a sincere and thorough examination by the sultan, his ministers and priests would immediately reveal its fraudulent nature, and they would easily be able to vanquish it.

What were they afraid of finding out by an open and sincere investigation?

Bahá'u'lláh wrote, "If this Cause be of God, no man can prevail against it; and if it be not of God, the divines [religious leaders] amongst you . . . will surely suffice to overpower it."[11]

Sulṭán 'Abdu'l-'Azíz was not interested in investigating anything Bahá'u'lláh might have to say. He was only interested in silencing Him. The sooner the better. The sultan had signed the edict banishing Bahá'u'lláh to the fortress of 'Akká so that he might put an end to His memory.

Even at that late date, Bahá'u'lláh was still trying to open the eyes of the king and the clergy by showing them the remarkable fulfillment of the promises from their own holy books. Bahá'u'lláh had been brought into the "Strong City" hailed by David by the edict of the sultan. Bahá'u'lláh pointed out that this was one of the least prophecies fulfilled by the acts of His enemies. Bahá'u'lláh said, simply and bluntly, to leave it to God and history to judge between them.

*Soon will We . . . lay hold on the Chief
who ruleth the land.*

A Roll of Drums

Sulṭán 'Abdu'l-'Azíz, the "self-styled vicar of the Prophet of Islám and the absolute ruler of a mighty empire" was "the first among the Oriental monarchs to sustain the impact of God's retributive justice."[12]

Bahá'u'lláh was not content to send only a verbal warning to the king of Turkey and his ministers. He also put it in writing. In forceful, unmistakable language, for all men to see, Bahá'u'lláh foretold their imminent downfall.

The prime minister, 'Alí Páshá; the foreign minister, Fu'ád Páshá; and the Persian ambassador, Mírzá Ḥusayn Khán, had all conspired in securing Bahá'u'lláh's successive banishments. Fu'ád Páshá was described by Bahá'u'lláh as the "instigator" of the fourth and final banishment to the prison of 'Akká. Fu'ád Páshá, to satisfy his foreign policy aims with relation to Persia, encouraged his fellow conspirator, 'Alí Páshá, to excite the fears and suspicions of Sulṭán 'Abdu'l-'Azíz. The sultan needed little encouragement. There was nothing vague or ambiguous about the words Bahá'u'lláh addressed to these ministers. It was an open challenge. Bahá'u'lláh directed it specifically to the ministers of the Turkish state. He warned them, and through them all leaders in a similar position of authority, about what would happen to those who were unjust and unscrupulous in their discharge of public trust: "It behoveth you, O Ministers of State, to keep the precepts of God . . . and to be of them who are guided aright. . . . Ye shall, erelong, discover the consequences of that which ye shall have done in this vain life, and shall be repaid for them."[13]

Bahá'u'lláh added the following words: "The days of your life shall roll away, and all the things with which ye are occupied and of which ye boast yourselves shall perish. . . . This is the day that shall inevitably come upon you, the hour that none can put back."[14]

Fu'ád Páshá was the first to feel the sting of requital. Within a year following Bahá'u'lláh's arrival at the prison-city of 'Akká, the foreign minister was struck down while on a trip to Paris, and he died at Nice, his plotting and ambitions perishing with him.

Bahá'u'lláh directed a second letter to the Turkish prime minister, 'Alí Páshá. He described that minister as the type of leader who in every age denounces and persecutes the Messengers of God. 'Alí Páshá, like Násiri'd-Dín Sháh of Persia, regarded himself as the hope of Turkey. His modernization program was to make the ramshackle empire a powerful nation. Far from weakening the sultan's dictatorship, this program would give the government still greater control.

He foretold the ruin of the prime minister and warned 'Alí Páshá not to be misled because of his present authority and high position, but to meditate on the significant premature death of his colleague. Bahá'u'lláh foreshadowed the calamities that would soon strike both the prime minister and the sultan himself. Bahá'u'lláh wrote openly of those forthcoming tragedies so that all the world might know that He had clearly predicted their downfall. Bahá'u'lláh wrote, "Soon will We dismiss the one ['Alí Páshá] who was like unto him [Fu'ád Páshá] and will lay hold on their Chief [Sultán 'Abdu'l-'Azíz] who ruleth the land."[15]

The prophecy was dramatically fulfilled. Without warning, 'Alí Páshá was suddenly shorn of all his power. He was summarily dismissed from office and shortly afterward died in complete oblivion. The political career that was to be the "hope of Turkey" had been short-lived.

Bahá'u'lláh also prophesied concerning the city of Adrianople. He described the tragedies that would befall the city and its peoples because of the neglect of justice not only by the king and his ministers, but by the people themselves.

Bahá'u'lláh's words now echo like a roll of drums: "The day is approaching when the Land of Mystery [Adrianople], and what is beside it shall be changed, and shall pass out of the hands of the king, and commotions shall appear, and the voice of lamentation shall be raised . . . by reason of that which hath befallen these captives at the hands of the hosts of oppression."[16]

Another of His prophecies foretold, "The course of things shall be altered, and conditions shall wax so grievous, that the very sands on the desolate hills will moan, and the trees on the mountain will weep, and blood will flow out of all things. Then wilt thou behold the people in sore distress."[17]

These words pointed out to 'Abdu'l-'Azíz that he, like his fellow-rulers, had time and time again ignored the needs and requirements of this present day. But the ruler was unmoved by the sufferings of his people. He was totally uninterested in any suggestions for reform that came from the pen of the Prisoner.

In order that the sultan should have no doubt whatsoever about the meaning of His words, Bahá'u'lláh stated, "Soon will He [God] seize you in His wrathful anger, and sedition will be stirred up in your midst, and your dominions will be disrupted. Then will ye bewail and lament, and will find no one to help or succor you."[18]

Like those of Napoleon III and other monarchs, this prophecy was fulfilled with terrifying swiftness. 'Abdu'l-'Azíz's misrule, of which his mistreatment of Bahá'u'lláh was a classic example, drove elements in the empire to desperation. They were not inclined, as Bahá'u'lláh was, to trust in God for redress.

We noted earlier in this book the events that followed. Without warning a palace revolution overthrew the imperial government. The sultan, whose very person was regarded as sacred, was seized by rude hands and imprisoned. The revolutionaries deposed him in favor of his nephew, 'Abdu'l-Ḥamíd, whom they believed they could rule.

The one remaining problem was what to do with the fallen monarch. The once all-powerful head of church and state had become merely an embarrassment.

The problem was solved in the same way that 'Abdu'l-'Azíz had solved his own problems. Early one morning the wretched king heard footsteps enter the room in which he was held. They were the last thing he heard.

Fear God, inhabitants of the city.

The Sixth Kingdom Falls

Through the reign of 'Abdu'l-Ḥamíd II uprisings increased in both intensity and violence. Finally, in 1909, an army sent by the Young Turks of Salonika marched in revenge upon the capital. It punished all who had opposed its plans for reform and took steps to deal with the new sultan.

'Abdu'l-Ḥamíd was deserted by his friends and condemned by his subjects. He was already hated by his fellow sovereigns of Europe. The sultan was forced to abdicate his throne and, like 'Abdu'l-'Azíz, was made a prisoner of the state before being sent into perpetual exile.

Thus, 'Abdu'l-Ḥamíd II, as had his uncle before him, suffered the same punishments that they had inflicted upon Bahá'u'lláh and His family. An even more terrible fate awaited the imperial ministers who had encouraged the kings in their injustice and had profited handsomely in the course of doing so.

On one single day in 1909, no less than thirty-one leading ministers and officials were arrested and condemned to the gallows. Among the thirty-one were some of the most notorious enemies of Bahá'u'lláh's Faith.

Constantinople itself, which had been honored as the splendid metropolis of the Roman Empire, and which had been made the capital of the Ottoman government, was abandoned as a capital city by the revolution. The city was stripped of its pomp and glory. Even its ancient name was dropped in favor of the colloquial "Istanbul." Ankara became the new capital.

The fate of Constantinople brought sharply to mind Bahá'u'lláh's words. He had spoken of the condition in which He found the city of Constantinople and its peoples when He arrived there as a Prisoner: "We found, upon Our arrival in the City, its governors and elders as children gathered about and disporting themselves with clay. . . . Our inner eye wept sore over them, and over their transgressions and their total disregard of the thing for which they were created."[19]

There was none to listen among the people of Constantinople. Bahá'u'lláh warned that the city would feel the fire of divine reprisal. "God, assuredly, dominateth the lives of them that wronged Us, and is well aware of their doings. He will, most certainly, lay hold on them for their sins. He, verily, is the fiercest of avengers."[20]

Constantinople lost in theory, as well as in fact, the position held well-nigh uninterruptedly for six centuries—that of the headship of a vast empire. The Ottoman Empire was ended. The revolutionaries were determined that the capital should be dishonored as well.

"No longer," they announced, "will Constantinople exact a tragic tribute of lives and treasure."

The mosques of the capital were deserted. The pride and joy of them all, the peerless St. Sophia, was converted into a museum. The Arabic tongue, the language of Muḥammad, was banished from the land.

Bahá'u'lláh's words ring clearly for those who have "ears to hear":

O Spot that art situate on the shores of the two seas [Constantinople]! The throne of tyranny hath, verily, been established upon thee, and the flame of hatred hath been kindled within thy bosom. . . . We behold in thee the foolish ruling over the wise, and darkness vaunting itself against the light. Thou art indeed filled with manifest pride. Hath thine outward splendor made thee vainglorious? By Him Who is the Lord of mankind! It shall soon perish, and thy daughters and thy widows and all the kindreds that dwell within thee shall lament. Thus informeth thee the All-Knowing, the All-Wise.[21]

How similar are Bahá'u'lláh's words to those that the persecuted Christ pronounced against Jerusalem "because thou knowest not the time of thy visitation."

The break was final and complete. The new capital of Turkey was transferred to Ankara. Constantinople, the "Dome of Islám," hailed by Constantine as the "New Rome," high-ranking metropolis of both Rome and Christendom, "revered as the seat of the caliphs" of Islam, was relegated to the station of a provincial city, was stripped of all its pomp and glory, "its soaring and slender minarets standing sentinel at the grave of so much vanished splendor and power."[22]

The sixth kingdom had fallen.

12 ❧ THE PRISON OPENS

No need to ask in Whose presence I stood.

Mount Carmel

Long before the extinction of the Ottoman Empire, the Prisoner of 'Akká had won the spiritual battle over His persecutors. The slander spread against Him by fearful or ambitious politicians in Constantinople had been able to prejudice the people and officials in 'Akká against Bahá'u'lláh before His arrival. Now, however, these same people had several years of direct experience with their Visitor.

His patience, His forbearance, and His wisdom had captivated the hardest hearts. Although few had even the dimmest conception of His mission, they regarded Bahá'u'lláh as a saint Whose presence was a blessing to the entire province.

The decree of banishment had never been repealed, but it had become a dead letter. Bahá'u'lláh was still nominally a prisoner, but the doors of the prison-city had been opened to Him by the officials in 'Akká who had come to know His true worth.

Bahá'u'lláh was at last free to walk on Mount Carmel. There He chose the site for the future shrine of His Herald, the Báb. Bahá'u'lláh arranged for the sacred remains of the Báb to be brought from Persia to the Holy Land.

Gradually, all elements of the population began to recognize Bahá'u'lláh's innocence of the crimes imputed to Him. Slowly the true spirit of His teachings penetrated through the "hard crust of their indifference and bigotry."[1]

The leading clergyman of 'Akká, Shaykh Maḥmúd, a man notorious for his bigotry, became converted to the Faith of

Bahá'u'lláh. He was fired with enthusiasm to compile all the many traditional prophecies from the writings of Islam concerning the significance of the city of 'Akká and its "Visitor." In more recent years, clergymen of all faiths have followed his example.

Men of letters, Christians and Jews as well as Muslims, sought His presence. Professor E. G. Browne of Cambridge University visited Bahá'u'lláh and was granted four successive interviews. He wrote of those hours, saying: "It was, in truth, a strange and moving experience, but one whereof I despair of conveying any save the feeblest impression."[2] Professor Browne declared that he underwent unparalleled spiritual joys. Perhaps men might disbelieve his words, Browne said, but if they ever came in contact with the spirit of Bahá'u'lláh, it would be an experience they would remember all the days of their lives.

Browne described one of his interviews with Bahá'u'lláh in these words: "The face of Him on Whom I gazed I can never forget, though I cannot describe it. . . . No need to ask in Whose presence I stood, as I bowed myself before One Who is the object of a devotion and love which kings might envy and emperors sigh for in vain!"[3]

He will break the yoke from off the necks of men.

The Center of the Covenant

Bahá'u'lláh passed from this world in His home outside the city of 'Akká on May 29, 1892. His mission had been fulfilled. Although not even His followers were aware of its extent, He had laid the foundations of a worldwide community that would provide the pattern for the "new order in human relations" that the kings had so tragically rejected.

The people of 'Akká knew only that they had lost something from their midst that was irreplaceable. A huge crowd of people from all religions and all walks of life thronged the fields that surrounded Bahá'u'lláh's dwelling. An eyewitness wrote, "a multitude of the inhabitants of 'Akká and of the neighboring villages . . . could be seen weeping, beating upon their heads and crying aloud their grief."

Bahá'u'lláh, in His own written Will and Testament, appointed 'Abdu'l-Bahá (a title meaning "Servant of Bahá'u'lláh") as the interpreter of His teachings in a document called the Kitáb-i-'Ahd ("The Book of My Covenant"). Bahá'u'lláh made 'Abdu'l-Bahá the center of that Covenant.

'Abdu'l-Bahá took up Bahá'u'lláh's appeal to the leaders and peoples of the world. He traveled extensively throughout Europe and America in 1911 and 1912 trying to awaken humanity to the dangers threatening it.

Upon arrival at the prison-city of 'Akká, Bahá'u'lláh is reported to have said to 'Abdu'l-Bahá, "Now I concentrate on My work writing commands and counsels for the world of the future; to thee I leave the province of talking with and ministering to the people."[4]

The book of Psalms spoke of such a "Covenant" that would be established for "all generations" by the Lord of Hosts in the day when God would "scatter thine enemies" and "beat down his foes." Psalms declared of that day, "I have made a covenant with my chosen. . . . Also I will make him my first-born, higher than the kings of the earth . . . and my covenant shall stand fast with him. . . . It shall be established forever as the moon."[5]

'Abdu'l-Bahá was not a Messenger or "Manifestation" of God as were Bahá'u'lláh, Christ, and the other founders of the great religions. His role in spiritual history is, in an important sense, a mystery. On the one hand 'Abdu'l-Bahá's life is the perfect example for those who have recognized Bahá'u'lláh. It is the proof that Bahá'u'lláh's teachings are the sane and creative way for people to live in the new age.

On the other hand, 'Abdu'l-Bahá is also the architect of the system of administrative institutions conceived and outlined by Bahá'u'lláh. 'Abdu'l-Bahá superintended the formation of the first of these democratically elected bodies on the pattern designed by Bahá'u'lláh. For the first time in history, a Messenger of God has brought not only spiritual teachings and social principles, but also model institutions.

It is because of this unique role conferred on 'Abdu'l-Bahá by Bahá'u'lláh's own pen that He is so revered and loved by Bahá'ís everywhere.

The story of the arrival of Bahá'u'lláh, at Mount Carmel in the Holy Land, there to establish this covenant with humanity for all time, is so beautiful and powerful that it is impossible not to share also the echo of Isaiah to the words of the book of Psalms above.

The greatest of the Hebrew prophets proclaimed,

And the Redeemer shall come to Zion. . . . This is my covenant with them, saith the Lord. . . . Arise, shine; for thy light is come, and the glory of the Lord [Bahá'u'lláh] is risen upon thee . . . darkness shall cover the earth, and gross darkness the people: but the Lord shall arise upon thee, and his glory shall be seen upon thee. . . . For the nation and kingdom that will not serve thee shall perish; yea, those nations shall be utterly wasted . . . and thou shalt know that I the Lord am thy Savior and thy Redeemer.[6]

In 'Akká, the persecutions that had begun under 'Abdu'l-'Azíz reached their culmination under his successor, 'Abdu'l-Ḥamíd II, before the fall of the Ottoman monarchy. 'Abdu'l-Bahá refused to allow these new threats to interfere with His assistance to the ill and the destitute. Each day He visited the orphan, the sick, and the downtrodden. Throughout His life, He serenely refused to allow His troubles to prevent Him from visiting in person those souls who needed His help.

One night early in the winter of 1907, 'Abdu'l-Bahá had a dream. He told His friends about it. He had seen a ship cast anchor off 'Akká. From it flew a few birds. When they approached, 'Abdu'l-Bahá saw that they resembled sticks of dynamite. The birds flew toward Him and circled above His head. 'Abdu'l-Bahá was standing in the midst of a great multitude of the frightened people of 'Akká. Suddenly, the "birds" returned to their ship without exploding.

A few days later a ship appeared on the horizon and anchored in the Bay of Haifa. It had brought from Constantinople another imperial investigation commission. It consisted of four officers, headed by one, 'Arif Bey. This commission was invested with plenary powers to summarily dispose of 'Abdu'l-Bahá in any way they deemed fit. Among the commission's members were outspoken enemies of Bahá'u'lláh and His Faith.

All telegraph and postal services in Haifa were immediately seized. The commission dismissed any official suspected of being friendly with 'Abdu'l-Bahá, including the governor of the city. They placed guards over 'Abdu'l-Bahá's house. Encouraged by this show of force, 'Abdu'l-Bahá's enemies flocked to the commission sessions to do their part in assuring His downfall. Even some of the poor, whom He had so long and so bountifully succored, now forsook Him because of their fear of reprisals.

Once again wild reports about 'Abdu'l-Bahá's fate spread through Haifa and 'Akká: 'Abdu'l-Bahá was to be taken on shipboard as a prisoner; He might be cast into the ocean at sea, or banished to the sands of Africa, or even nailed to the city gates of 'Akká.

'Abdu'l-Bahá, His tranquillity unshaken, told some of the Bahá'ís who still remained at 'Akká: "The meaning of the dream I dreamt is now clear. . . . Please God this dynamite will not explode."[7]

*I will work a wonder which ye will not
believe even though it be told to you.*

God's Gun

One evening, just before sunset, the ship, which had been ly-
ing off Haifa, weighed anchor. It headed for 'Akká. The news
spread rapidly. The commission had boarded the vessel. It was
expected that they would stop at 'Akká long enough to take
'Abdu'l-Bahá on board.

Anguish seized the family of 'Abdu'l-Bahá. The few believers who were left in the city wept with grief at the thought of
separation from Him. 'Abdu'l-Bahá could be seen at that tragic
hour calmly walking alone and silent in the courtyard of His
house.

With the setting sun, the sky darkened and the lights of the
ship could be seen clearly. Suddenly the ship changed her
course. She swung about and was now obviously sailing directly for Constantinople!

The dynamite had not exploded! Rather, dynamite of a
different kind had been detonated. In the capital city, the
Young Turks had revolted and swept aside all royal resistance.
'Abdu'l-Ḥamíd II had been deposed, and a puppet-king was
set up in his place. The ship that was to carry 'Abdu'l-Bahá to
certain death instead conveyed those who condemned 'Abdu'l-
Bahá back to Constantinople, to their own destruction.

The gun that had touched off the Young Turk Rebellion
not only removed the threat from over 'Abdu'l-Bahá's head,
but it also freed Him from an imprisonment that had lasted

for over fifty years. The imprisonment had begun when 'Abdu'l-Bahá was but a child of nine. It ended when He was sixty-four.

After gaining his freedom, 'Abdu'l-Bahá carried the Faith of His father to Africa, Europe, and America. These apostolic journeys will remain forever unique in the annals of religious history. Imagine! The son of a Messenger of God visiting and speaking in cathedrals, churches, synagogues, schools, universities, addressing lord mayors, presidents, educators, philosophers, entering the homes of millionaires and the slum-dwellings of the poor!

'Abdu'l-Bahá was entertained by princes, maharajas, and noblemen. He spoke to leading clergymen in both England and America, to Theosophists, agnostics, materialists, spiritualists, Christian Scientists, social reformers, Hindus, Sufis, Muslims, Buddhists, and Zoroastrians, as well as Catholics, Protestants, and Jews.

Secretaries of state, ambassadors, congressmen, members of parliament, ministers of state, presidents of universities, famous scholars, military leaders, and socialites all met Him and heard His message of unity.

For eight long months 'Abdu'l-Bahá traveled coast to coast in the United States and Canada proclaiming His Father's Faith from pulpit, platform, and press. Whatever the future may hold, it will never be possible for people to say they did not have the opportunity to hear about the Revelation of God to our age.

Why did not millions instead of thousands listen and believe?

Perhaps a clue can be found in the book of Habakkuk, who prophesied that the "knowledge of the Lord" (Bahá'u'lláh) would "cover the earth as the "waters cover the sea." Habakkuk also declared, "Behold . . . regard, and wonder marvelously: for I will work a work in your days which ye will not believe, though it be told you."[8]

During the First World War, 'Abdu'l-Bahá wrote His history-making Tablets of the Divine Plan, which called on the followers of Bahá'u'lláh to carry the message of world unity and social justice to every corner of the globe, however remote. They responded by the thousands. The community of Bahá'u'lláh is now established in more than one hundred thousand centers in over 236 independent nations and major territories.

It is little wonder that students of past scriptures should begin to become interested in words of Daniel, which have found remarkable fulfillment in the story of Bahá'u'lláh. Not only did Daniel predict the overthrow of kings, he also prophesied, "And in the days of these [wicked] kings shall the God of heaven set up a kingdom, which shall never be destroyed . . . it shall stand forever."[9]

These things Daniel pictured as taking place in a period that many Christian Bible scholars have said must have begun in 1844, the year of the birth of the Bahá'í Faith.

'Abdu'l-Bahá has said of the downfall of 'Abdu'l-Ḥamíd: "God removed the chains from my neck and placed them around the neck of 'Abdu'l-Ḥamíd. It was done suddenly— not in a long time—in a moment as it were. The same hour that the Young Turks declared liberty, the Committee of Union and Progress set me free. They lifted the chains from my neck and threw them around the neck of 'Abdu'l-Ḥamíd. That which he did to me was inflicted on him."[10]

Of the weapon that had fired off the Young Turk revolt in such forceful terms, 'Abdu'l-Bahá said, "That was God's gun."

———— ✒ ————

*The face of Him on Whom I gazed,
I can never forget.*

The Envy of Kings

This was not, however, the end of the story.

During World War I, the Turkish commander-in-chief of the military forces in the Holy Land was Jamál Páshá. This suspicious and ruthless officer established a harsh and complete military dictatorship. In such a regime there was no place for One Who taught that all men were one and that justice is the Will of God for our age.

Jamál Páshá subjected 'Abdu'l-Bahá to repeated insults and indignities and threatened to destroy the tomb of Bahá'u'lláh. He openly boasted that if the Turkish Army was forced to evacuate Haifa, he would "crucify 'Abdu'l-Bahá on Mount Carmel."

The British followers of Bahá'u'lláh were alarmed when this news reached them. They enlisted the aid of some of the cabinet members, including Lord Curzon, who had written in 1892, the year of the death of Bahá'u'lláh, praising the "sublime" devotion of the early followers of His Faith.

Through Lord Curzon's intervention, Lord Lamington wrote to the Foreign Office explaining the importance of 'Abdu'l-

Bahá's position. On the day of the receipt of this letter, Lord Balfour sent a message to General Allenby in Egypt. He instructed the general to "extend every protection and consideration to 'Abdu'l-Bahá, His family and His friends."

Allenby's army entered Palestine and Jerusalem ahead of schedule. His surprise entry routed the Turkish forces.

Christian Arabs, unaware of the significance of Bahá'u'lláh's Faith or of His words to the rulers of Turkey, pointed proudly to the protection that God had given to them and to the Holy Land in that critical hour. It was the Hand of God raised up to save them, they said. It came through General Allenby, they explained, whose very name showed him to be an instrument of the Lord. The name "Allenby" was akin to "Al Nabi," which in Arabic means "The Prophet." For half a century these same people had remained unaware of the significance of the presence of Bahá'u'lláh and His Faith in their midst.

General Allenby issued instructions to the officer in command at Haifa to insure 'Abdu'l-Bahá's safety. After the capture of Haifa, Allenby sent a cable to London. He requested the authorities to "notify the world that 'Abdu'l-Bahá is safe."

The plot of the Turkish commander, Jamál Páshá, was frustrated. Defeated in battle, he fled from the country. He was later slain while traveling as an exile in the Caucasus.

The fate of Jamál Páshá was only a minor footnote in the turbulent history of the period. Even the collapse of the Turkish regime in the Holy Land seemed somewhat anticlimactic.

Of far greater importance was the response of the world to the Message of God. That Message had been proclaimed in four continents as a result of the widely publicized travels and writings of 'Abdu'l-Bahá. The most powerful of the despots who had stood between humankind and the Messenger of unity had been swept aside. New governments and new nations had come into existence.

Many of the leading statesmen, reformers, and thinkers of this new world had met and talked with 'Abdu'l-Bahá. Many of them had paid extravagant tribute to His wisdom and character, and to the vision in His father's Revelation.

Now the opportunity for action had come. Republican governments and constitutional monarchies held the power formerly held by the Hohenzollerns and Romanovs. What would they do with it?

13 ☙ FALLING KINGDOMS EVERYWHERE

Twenty years have passed, O Kings!

Falling Kingdoms Everywhere

The words of Bahá'u'lláh and 'Abdu'l-Bahá made it clear that it was not merely the recipients of specific letters who were summoned by God. All the kings and rulers were responsible for the trust that they had accepted. And the day had come when this trust must be answered by acts of justice.

To no other group did this apply so specifically as it did to kings. The subsequent decline in the fortunes of royalty and the disappearance of so many thrones can be understood only in·relationship to their neglect of the Message of God. Bahá'u'lláh warned them of the great loss they would sustain if they did not heed the counsel given them: "O Kings of the earth! . . . Ye examined not His Cause when to do so would have been better for you than all that the sun shineth upon, could you but perceive it."[1]

Bahá'u'lláh searched in vain for that great leader of men who would be willing to make any sacrifice necessary in order to uphold justice; not for the East or the West, the rich or the poor, the light or the dark, the Jew or the Gentile, but for all men who lived in this one homeland, the planet.

Bahá'u'lláh extolled the greatness of such a leader of men: "How great is the blessedness that awaiteth the king who will arise to aid My Cause. . . . Such a king is the very eye of mankind. . . . the fountainhead of blessings unto the whole world."[2]

Through half a lifetime Bahá'u'lláh waited patiently for such a king or leader to arise. He longed to witness in His own lifetime, if possible, the fruits of such heroic action. The world, He declared, could have become another world, and the people another people, if they had responded to His call.

Instead of the "Most Great Peace," humankind would now have to content himself with the "Lesser Peace." Humanity, because of its lack of response would have to win its way to the goal of a united and peaceful world through suffering. No king, however, and no nation arose in answer to His call. At last Bahá'u'lláh was moved to declare, "Twenty years have passed, O kings . . . ye, nevertheless, have failed to stay the hand of the aggressor. For is it not your clear duty to restrain the tyranny of the oppressor, and to deal equitably with your subjects, that your high sense of justice may be fully demonstrated to all mankind?"[3]

The leaders of men had permitted the "wolves" to inflict "injustice" upon their "sheep." Therefore, the hour of retribution could be put off no longer. Bahá'u'lláh made a startling declaration. "Power," He announced, had been "seized" by God from the kings, and the "winds of despair" would soon "assail" them from every direction. Bahá'u'lláh wrote of those tyrant kings, saying, "They have been seized by their forelock, and yet know it not."[4]

Only two years expired between the time that Bahá'u'lláh's first letters to the kings were delivered and ignored and the time the first kingdom was overthrown. The French monarch, Napoleon III, who had twice repudiated Bahá'u'lláh's counsel, and who had deliberately insulted Him, was the first to be toppled from his throne. He was followed by an endless line of his fellow monarchs during the subsequent decades.

The following, in chronological order, is a partial list of significant events related to Bahá'u'lláh's historic pronouncements to the crowned heads of the world and of the fate that overtook some of the major kingdoms of the world.

Fall of the French Monarchy (1870)

Assassination of Sulṭán 'Abdu'l-'Azíz (1876)

Assassination of Náṣiri'd-Dín Sháh (1896)

Overthrow of Sulṭán 'Abdu'l-Ḥamíd II (1909)

Fall of the Portuguese Monarchy (1910)

Fall of the Chinese Monarchy (1911)

Fall of the Russian Monarchy (1917)

Fall of the German Monarchy (1918)

Fall of the Austrian Monarchy (1918)

Fall of the Hungarian Monarchy (1918)

Fall of the Turkish Monarchy (1922)

Fall of the Qájár Dynasty (1925)

Fall of the Spanish Monarchy (1931)

Fall of the Albanian Monarchy (1938)

Fall of the Serbian Monarchy (1941)

Fall of the Italian Monarchy (1946)

Fall of the Bulgarian Monarchy (1946)

Fall of the Romanian Monarchy (1947)

Fall of the Egyptian Monarchy (1952)

Fall of the Iraqi Monarchy (1958)

Fall of the Yemenite Monarchy (1962)

Vast and awesome is the spectacle that greets the eyes of those who survey the field over which the requiting wind of God has blown since the beginning of Bahá'u'lláh's mission.

Volumes have been written by historians and politicians on the subject of these falling empires. In vain, scholars have tried to explain this spectacle in terms political or historical forces alone.

Magazines and syndicated news articles have celebrated the glories of the Victorian and Edwardian ages with their colorful kings and unrivaled pageantry, but they have searched unavailingly to uncover the fateful forces that drove them to their end.

No one, when Bahá'u'lláh wrote His first letter from far-off Adrianople in 1867, could have foreseen the worldwide collapse of an institution that had been regarded as the central pillar of every civilization in history. The popular mind could not imagine a world without monarchies. No sane historian or political philosopher would have been prepared to make such a prediction.

It was left to the Messenger of God to announce publicly, and around the world, the long, final curtain-call of the kings.

——— ❧ ———

All the great houses shall have an end.

From the Top of Carmel

With the completion of Bahá'u'lláh's announcement to the kings, the great and dreadful Day foretold by Jeremiah had dawned and was rising towards the fury of its noonday heat. Jeremiah prophesied concerning the Day of the Promised One. He told us what God would do to the tyrant and unjust kings of the earth:

> Take the wine cup of this fury at my hand, and cause all the nations to whom I send thee, to drink it. . . . And all the kings of the north, far and near, one with another, and all the kingdoms of the world, which are upon the face of the earth. . . . Thou shalt say unto them, thus saith the Lord of hosts . . . drink ye, and be drunken, and spue, and fall and rise no more because of the sword which I will send among you. . . . Ye shall not be unpunished: for I will call for a sword upon all the inhabitants of the earth, saith the Lord of Hosts.[5]

The punishment was far advanced. Gone were the Houses of Hohenzollern, Hapsburg, Romanov, Bonaparte, 'Uthmán, and Qájár. Gone were most of the lesser dynasties and kingdoms that once ruled the earth. The "whirlwind" that Isaiah had promised would come and blow away kings and princes had now swept across the entire face of the earth.

Perhaps no Old Testament prophet had foreseen that coming royal disaster more clearly than Amos. It was this same

Amos who had so accurately described the physical events that took place at the time the Báb, the Herald of the Bahá'í Faith, faced a death regiment of 750 muskets.[6]

Amos prophesied, as had Isaiah before Him, that in the "day of the whirlwind," the "king" and "his princes" would go into captivity. There would be a "famine" and a "thirst" for hearing the "words of the Lord." A disillusioned mankind, godless and materialistic, would helplessly "run to and fro" in search of the "words" of God, never finding them.[7]

In that day, Amos declared, the Lord would "roar" from Zion and the "top of Carmel" would "wither" at His presence.[8] Bahá'u'lláh's words now echo ominously through empty palaces: "O kings of the earth. . . . If ye pay no heed unto the counsels that, in peerless and unequivocal language, We have revealed in this Tablet, Divine chastisement shall assail you from every direction, and the sentence of His [God's] justice shall be pronounced against you. On that day ye shall have no power to resist Him, and shall recognize your own impotence. Have mercy on yourselves and on those beneath you."[9]

It is the astonishing assertion of God's Messenger to our age that the time for the punishment of all forms of aggression had come. No aggressor, no matter how powerful, can cope with the forces loose in the world: "God hath not blinked, nor will He ever blink His eyes at the tyranny of the oppressor. More particularly in this Revelation hath He visited each and every tyrant with His vengeance."[10]

From His captivity in 'Akká, that "door of hope" promised by Hosea, Bahá'u'lláh, in the final years of His life, surveyed the world, its peoples, and their response to His summons. After many long years of continuous entreaty, Bahá'u'lláh was able to say with assurance, although no doubt with sadness:

"We verily have not fallen short of Our duty to exhort men, and to deliver that whereunto I was bidden by God, the Almighty, the All-Praised. Had they hearkened unto Me, they would have beheld the earth another earth."[11]

The proofs had been delivered. The prophecies had been fulfilled. The seals were opened. The Promised One of every religion, nation, and people had discharged His God-given mission in a global proclamation, a worldwide announcement such as the eyes of mortal man had never before witnessed.

Bahá'u'lláh, in the closing days of His earthly mission declared, "Is there any excuse left for anyone in this Revelation? No, by God, the Lord of the Mighty Throne! My signs have encompassed the earth, and My power enveloped all mankind."[12]

14 ⚘ AND ALL THE KING'S MEN

Soon will the present-day order be rolled up.

The Legacy of the Kings

The Hapsburgs and Hohenzollerns are gone, but their legacy remains. And, alas, all humankind are their heirs.

Tragically, it has not been only kings who have failed to respond to the needs of a new age and to its divine Spokesman. When the First World War ended, only one head of state arose to champion the kind of world that Bahá'u'lláh had envisioned.

Years earlier, in His announcement to the kings, Bahá'u'lláh had called for the formation of an international tribunal to judge between the nations. In the middle of the nineteenth century the idea seemed revolutionary.

Even more revolutionary were the features that He proposed: "The rulers and kings of the earth must needs attend it, and, participating in its deliberations, must consider such ways and means as will lay the foundations of the world's Great Peace."[1]

The tribunal was not to be merely a conference, a place for discussion. It was to have powers to enforce peace, powers derived from the cooperative action of all governments: "Be united O kings of the earth. . . . Should any one among you take up arms against another, rise ye all against him, for this is naught but manifest justice."[2]

During the 1919 peace conferences, Woodrow Wilson, president of the United States, called for a League of Nations to assure the permanent peace of the world. The president's daughter showed keen interest in the new Revelation. Whether through this link, or merely because his own ideals were so closely attuned to the spirit of the age, President Wilson called his fellow statesmen to join with him in this first modest experiment in international control.

What followed is a familiar and tragic story. Betrayed by the diplomatic ambitions of other nations, cruelly disappointed by the attitude adopted by many of his own countrymen, this "tragically unappreciated" statesman saw his dream wrecked.[3] His own life was given in a fruitless attempt to secure the support of the United States for the newly created world body.

When the League came into existence, it lacked the teeth to make its decisions effective. Long before night fell on Europe in 1939, the "League of Peace" had become an international mockery.

Bahá'u'lláh's words to "the elected representatives of the people in every land" contain ominous and very clear warnings to the successors of the monarchies: "Regard the world as the human body which, though at its creation whole and perfect, hath been afflicted, through various causes, with grave disorders and maladies. . . . Its sickness waxed more severe, as it fell under the treatment of ignorant physicians, who gave full rein to their personal desires."[4]

The reminder of the ruin brought by the reckless military adventures of the fallen kings fell on deaf ears. Throughout the world the only solutions advanced for the problems in which society has been steadily sinking have been political, or at best social and economic. Until very recently all suggestions that the roots of the disorder are spiritual have been treated with impatience or ridicule.

How ominous, in the age since Hiroshima, are these words of the Prisoner of 'Akká, uttered a century ago, "Strange and astonishing things exist in the earth but they are hidden from the minds and the understanding of men. These things are capable of changing the whole atmosphere of the earth and their contamination would prove lethal."[5]

And finally: "Oppression will envelop the world. And following a universal convulsion, the sun of justice will rise from the horizon of the unseen realm."[6] "Soon will the present-day order be rolled up, and a new one spread out in its stead. Verily, thy Lord speaketh the truth, and is the Knower of things unseen."[7]

How odd that our civilization should have left the spiritual realm almost totally unexplored.

A New View of History

And what about us? What about the millions of people who make up the "mankind" that Bahá'u'lláh sought to protect from the ignorance of kings and despots?

Bahá'u'lláh's message is directed not only to governments but also to each individual human being. How odd that our civilization, which harnessed the atom, probed space, discovered so many miraculous secrets of nature, and made so many brilliant advancements in all the sciences, should have left the spiritual realm almost totally unexplored.

How did it happen that humanity, with its gigantic resources and unequaled brilliance, missed the most important truth of all: a moral and spiritual understanding of history?

The real purpose of life, the Bahá'í teachings point out, is the development of a praiseworthy character. The building of moral and ethical virtues is the true business of life for both people and nations. Anything that advances this goal is of value and should be encouraged. Anything that hampers, delays, or prevents it is useless and should be discarded. All life revolves around this goal. It is the reason for existence. Every event in life depends for its ultimate usefulness and value on its direct or indirect connection with this main purpose. It is worthwhile if it forwards this great theme. It is worthless if it does not.

Any philosophy that does not advance in some way this perspective of life is futile. Any person who devotes himself to something else, such as acquiring wealth, seeking pleasure or luxury, or chasing ambition, reputation, or conquest, and thinks of that goal as having in itself an independent value and importance separate from the spiritual and moral motivation of his life is, sooner or later, doomed to disillusionment and unhappiness.

Such a person is without a real purpose in life. He will be prone to depression and self-destruction in one form or another. He will gradually destroy himself physically or morally or both, through despair or through the excessive physical pleasure by which he seeks in vain to escape his destiny.

That is the tragedy that is taking place on a planetary scale today.

No one loves us. Not our mothers, our fathers, our children, our wives, our husbands, our sweethearts. No one.

Our families and friends love only the inner qualities we possess—kindness, generosity, compassion, tenderness, love, justice, fairness, gentleness, consideration; these are the things they love. As we increase these qualities in our lives, their love for us increases. As we lose these virtues, their love for us withers and dies away.

And what is true of individuals is also true of nations or civilizations. To acquire these inward moral and ethical virtues is the real business of life, for both the individual soul and society.

Every other goal is meaningless by comparison.

The world today has lost most of these virtues. It continues to lose more. Both men and nations are drifting on the tide of empty materialism. Something must reverse the current. That is why Bahá'u'lláh has come. That is the mission of His Faith.

The churches can find no remedy because they have lost their Divine Physician, Christ. His Spirit left them over a century ago when He returned in the glory of the Father, Bahá'u'lláh, and the churches and their leaders turned their back on Him—just as they had the first time. The same is true of each of the other great religions of the past.

Had this not been the case, the clergy of the world's religions would have responded to the Message for which they claimed they had been yearning for centuries. Because the Messenger spoke directly to them, individually and collectively, as clearly as He addressed the kings.

He spoke, for example, to Pope Pius IX. And the story of that brief encounter and its reverberations in modern history may well be the most dramatic chapter of the entire spiritual drama.

Bahá'u'lláh told the pope that He was the Father Who had been promised by Christ, the Son. The very One the pope was awaiting; the One in Whose Name the pontiff held his position.

There has been only a century of silence from the church. But the seeds were sown, and let us see what took place a hundred years later.

O Supreme Pontiff!

Echoes from the Past

How many Christians have made a study of the now famous pastoral letter of Pope John XXIII, the encylical *Pacem in Terris* ("Peace on Earth")? Most Protestants perhaps couldn't have cared less. But how many Catholics are aware of its contents?

For the origins of this encyclical, which had such far-reaching effects on the two-thousand-year-old Roman Catholic Church, we must turn back to the words Bahá'u'lláh addressed to Pope John's predecessor Pius IX in 1869.

Bahá'u'lláh told the pontiff bluntly that the "Father" had come as promised by the "Son," Jesus the Christ. Bahá'u'lláh said that He was that Father. The response was less than joyful.

Perhaps that attitude was understandable a hundred years ago—regrettable, but understandable. The world head of any religion is not likely to be stirred to his depths when his position of eminence is challenged—especially by such a seemingly preposterous claim, written from a penal-colony prison by a condemned exile.

Caiaphas didn't go into spasms of ecstasy when Christ told him He was the "Son of God." And he met Jesus face to face. Instead, he called Christ a blasphemer.

We can imagine then the reaction generated by Bahá'u'lláh's letter to the pope. No one even bothered to call Him a blasphemer, although His claim was even more presumptuous than Christ's. Nor did the Curia exhibit the annoyance and alarm that had been aroused among several of the kings. Instead, a curtain of silence descended around the entire subject.

Then, in the *exact year* and *exact month* of the *one hundredth anniversary of Bahá'u'lláh's Declaration* to the world proclaiming that the sacred promise in all the Holy Books had been fulfilled, Pope John XXIII issued his encyclical letter, which "received worldwide acclaim."

The praise was justified. Not only did the encylical deal with the problems facing the world, but Pope John himself was a true lover of his fellow man, a saintly human being.

In that encyclical, the supreme pontiff spoke of the following subjects:

World peace

A world community

Search after truth

Universal education

Equality between men and women

The oneness of humankind

The oneness of God

The harmony of science and religion

Disarmament

A warning concerning atomic energy

A spiritual solution to the economic problem

Do these ideas sound familiar?

They are one and all principles of the Bahá'í Faith. They are teachings and counsels that Bahá'u'lláh had given to the kings and religious leaders of the world more than a century previous. The pontiff finally spoke out, exactly *one hundred years afterward.*

How powerfully those words of Bahá'u'lláh, spoken so long ago to a pope in Rome, now ring through the halls of history after a century: "O Supreme Pontiff! Incline thine ear unto that which the Fashioner of moldering bones counseleth thee."[8]

Pope John XXIII, because of his sincere love of humanity and his wise guidance to a troubled world, received the Nobel Prize for peace. He was admired and lauded in all parts of the world by both public and press.

Yet he had no more than echoed, faintly at that, and only after a hundred years, the teachings of Bahá'u'lláh. He had done no more than to share with humanity ideals that had been denied to the world for a century by the leaders of men, both religious and secular.

What was Bahá'u'lláh's reward?

He was scourged, chained, banished and imprisoned for nearly half a century. He was denounced as an enemy of religion and civil order.

The most bitter and persistent of those denouncing His teachings, whether in Persia, Turkey, or the Near East, had been the clergy. The Muslim clergy indeed had taken the lead, but it is an unhappy fact that those who did most to spread these early slanders were Christians, missionaries who feared the loss of their jealously guarded flocks.

Their church, however, had only begun to experience the delayed effects of the Revelation they had so long awaited.

Emerge from your palace!

More Echoes from the Same Pen

It is almost impossible to turn to any great event taking place in the religious world today without tracing its inspiration to the words that Bahá'u'lláh addressed so long ago to the ecclesiastics of the nineteenth century.

How many Catholics are aware of the significance of the visit of Pope Paul VI to the United Nations? How many Christians are aware of the spiritual implications of the pope's visit to the World Council of Churches in Switzerland? Or to Kampala, Uganda? All of these events have their roots in Bahá'u'lláh's letter to Pope Piux IX.

Bahá'u'lláh called upon the pope to "arise in the name of thy Lord." He urged the Pope to "emerge" from his "palaces" and "speak forth the praises of thy Lord betwixt earth and heaven." Bahá'u'lláh urged Pope Pius IX to "sell the embellished ornaments" he possessed and "expend them in the path of God."[9]

Bahá'u'lláh was not asking the pope to do anything He had not already done Himself in a fuller measure.

When the hour came for Bahá'u'lláh to carry out the bidding of the Almighty, He was in the "hey-day of His life." Yet He flung aside "every consideration of earthly fame, wealth and position."[10] Bahá'u'lláh was a nobleman of the province of Núr in Persia. He had everything our world prizes so highly. Bahá'u'lláh cast them all aside, although He knew only too well where such a decision would lead Him.

During those hours when Pope Pius IX rode the crest of popularity and sovereignty, Bahá'u'lláh had fallen from the highest to the lowest estate, from wealth to poverty, from freedom to imprisonment. Bahá'u'lláh thanked God for such "tribulations" saying, "The throat Thou didst accustom to the touch of silk Thou hast, in the end, clasped with strong chains, and the body Thou didst ease with brocades and velvets Thou hast at last subjected to the abasement of a dungeon."[11]

Bahá'u'lláh now urged the pontiff to follow this example. He told the pope to leave his "palace" and to assist the Father, and to "proffer" His teachings to the "people of all faiths."[12]

In the prison-city from which Bahá'u'lláh sent His letter to Pius IX, He wrote, "The Ancient Beauty [Bahá'u'lláh] hath consented to be bound with chains that mankind may be released from its bondage, and hath accepted to be made a prisoner within this most mighty Stronghold that the whole world may attain unto true liberty. He hath drained to its dregs the cup of sorrow, that all the peoples of the earth may attain unto abiding joy, and be filled with gladness."[13]

Such tasks should have been the business of the pope as well. The pope declared himself to be the vicar of Christ on earth. Bahá'u'lláh told him that the Promised One Whom he awaited had come. The returned Christ was standing before his eyes.

Bahá'u'lláh warned the pope not to reject Him because His name was different than he expected: "O Pope . . . Beware lest any name debar thee from God. . . . Dwellest thou in palaces whilst He Who is the King of Revelation liveth in the most desolate of abodes? Leave them unto such as desire them, and set thy face with joy and delight toward the Kingdom."[14]

Pope Pius IX did none of these things. The pope was soon to suffer the same loss of his worldly kingdom as had the secular rulers.

In those days, Pius IX was a temporal as well as a spiritual king. As with his fellow monarchs, however, he found himself caught up in the forces released by the "Day of God." In 1870, only a year after Bahá'u'lláh had revealed His epistle to Pius IX, King Victor Emmanuel II suddenly declared war with the Papal States. The royalist troops had entered Rome and seized it.

The following morning, as the cannonade began, the pope ordered the white flag to be hoisted above the dome of St. Peter. The pope shut himself up in the buildings left to him and declared himself to be "the Prisoner of the Vatican."

"Rome, the 'Eternal City, on which rest twenty-five centuries of glory,' and over which the Popes had ruled in unchallengeable right for ten centuries, finally became the seat of the new kingdom, and the scene of that humiliation which Bahá'u'lláh had anticipated and which the Prisoner of the Vatican had imposed upon himself."[15]

The commands of God in the directive to the pope, however, remained to be carried out. The fall of Pius IX did not change the obligation on those who declared themselves the vicars on earth of Jesus Christ. Pope John XXIII was the first pontiff, unwittingly, to carry out the role assigned to the papacy. His successor, Pope Paul VI, had carried this response much further, and much less willingly. Paul VI answered Bahá'u'lláh's century-old "summons" to "emerge" from the

Lateran "palace" and go out "amidst the peoples of the world." He visited Africa, Asia, Latin America, North America and Europe, thus breaking with twenty centuries of papal tradition.

One of the most important visits of Pope Paul VI was to the United Nations headquarters in New York City. There he did "speak out" among the leaders of men. He did "exhort" them to "justice" and to be mindful of the things in the holy book of God.[16]

Why is this particular event interesting to the student of Bahá'u'lláh's story?

For the following reasons, to give only a few: Bahá'u'lláh, in His writings, called upon the kings and leaders to establish an international body such as the United Nations. Later, His son 'Abdu'l-Bahá visited New York City, and while there explained the significances of Bahá'u'lláh's Covenant with the peoples of the world. New York City, the United Nations' world headquarters, has been named in the Bahá'í writings as the "City of the Covenant" of Bahá'u'lláh. 'Abdu'l-Bahá also visited California. While in the shadow of San Francisco, 'Abdu'l-Baha said that California was worthy to raise the first banner of International Peace. In San Francisco, some thirty years after His visit, the United Nations Charter was written, and the blue and white flag of the United Nations, a symbol of peace, was created.

How remarkable that in this involuntary manner a pope had answered God's century-old "summons."

While addressing the United Nations, Pope Paul VI, like John XXIII before him, echoed the very principles that Bahá'u'lláh had given to the world so long ago.

It is a tragedy for us all that it took over a hundred years. It is a greater tragedy that the pontiff, a sincere and holy man, was far too late for his words to have any effect.

Only one thing could have made his address relevant. He could have repeated Bahá'u'lláh's words to his predecessor: "He Who is the Lord of Lords is come. . . . He hath stored away that which He chose in the vessels of justice, and cast into the fire that which befitteth it."[17]

The pope's rendezvous with history, however, was not yet complete. Two other specific tasks had been appointed to his office. His predecessors had let them pass, and God would wait no longer.

Impelled as by an unseen hand, he proceeded on the course laid out for him a hundred years earlier.

Enter into wedlock, O people, that ye may bring forth one who will make mention of Me amid My servants.

O Concourse of Priests!

Bahá'u'lláh invited Pius IX to visit Him in the Holy Land.

If the pope loved and remembered Christ, he would open his heart to Bahá'u'lláh.

"Reliance" on God would be the only "provision" he would need for such a journey.[18]

It was clear that if he were truly waiting, truly seeking, the pope would not fail to investigate a claim that had the stupendous moral authority that Bahá'u'lláh's reputation was now giving to His words. If the pope did not come himself, there were hundreds whom he could send.

The journey was never made. There was only silence from the church—a century of silence.

Then, one hundred years later, Pope Paul VI visited the Holy Land. Again breaking all precedent, and for reasons that were never made clear, he left Rome and visited the land to which the Messenger of God had summoned his predecessor.

Paul VI was accorded a huge welcome, similar to that which had greeted Emperor Franz Josef and Kaiser William I so long before him. It was hailed as a great event in the press. After 150 years of no pope leaving Italy, one had come at last to the Holy Land.

Bahá'u'lláh came as a prisoner and an exile, despised and imprisoned. The vicar who sat on His throne and held that seat of honor in the Promised One's name, against the day of His return, was showered with praise and blessings.

It was a century too late. The Promised One was no longer there. Nor did Pope Paul VI seek to investigate the flourishing center whose shrines and gardens covered the slope of Mount Carmel in memory of the Prisoner of 'Akká.

During the visit of Pope Paul VI to Israel, news arrived at the World Center of the Bahá'í Faith announcing that the teachings of Bahá'u'lláh were well established all over the world. (More than 2,100 tribes, races, and ethnic groups in more than one hundred thousand localities on the planet are enrolled under the banner of Bahá'u'lláh.)

This had been envisioned by Habakkuk: "For the earth shall be filled with the knowledge of the glory of the Lord, as the waters cover the sea."[19]

The press, television, and radio were all reporting the wrong story. But that had happened before, too.

There on the side of Mount Carmel stood the seat of that "Kingdom" which the pope and more than 500 million Catholics extolled daily in their prayers.

The Kingdom *had* come. God's Will *had* been done on earth as promised in the Lord's prayer. The Christ-promised Kingdom had appeared in the exact spot foretold in passage after passage from the holy book revered by the pope and his people. But, unhappily, neither Catholics nor Protestants were aware of it.

Surely the echo of Bahá'u'lláh's voice must have reverberated through those holy hills on the occasion of Pope Paul's visit. Like rolling thunder those words must have resounded through Zion, Jerusalem, Bethlehem, and Nazareth, where they were originally uttered:

O Pope! . . . Lo! The Father is come.[20]

O Concourse of patriarchs! He Whom ye were promised in the Tablets is come.[21]

O Concourse of archbishops! He Who is the Lord of all men hath appeared.[22]

O Concourse of bishops! . . . He Who is the Everlasting Father calleth aloud between earth and heaven.[23]

O Concourse of priests! Leave the bells, and come forth, then, from your churches. . . . The Lord is come in His great glory![24]

O Concourse of monks! . . . Come forth by My leave . . .
Thus biddeth you the King of the Day of Reckoning. . . .
Enter ye into wedlock, that after you someone may fill your
place.[25]

O Concourse of Christians! . . . Ye call upon Me, and are
heedless of My Revelation . . . O people of the Gospel! . . .
Verily, He (Jesus) said: "Come after Me, and I will make
you to become fishers of men." In this day, however, We
say: "Come ye after Me, that we may make you quickeners
of mankind."[26]

Ironically, Bahá'u'lláh's letter to Pope Pius IX had repeatedly warned the pontiff not to make the same mistake the
high priests and religious leaders made in the days of Christ.

Bahá'u'lláh wrote, "Thou, in truth, art one of the suns of
the heaven of His names. Guard thyself; lest darkness spread
its veils over thee, and fold thee away from His light."[27]

Christ Himself had warned against such a calamity. In the
chapter of Matthew in which Jesus gave so many proofs of the
time of His coming, He also warned that the sun shall be
"darkened, and the moon shall not give her light, and the
stars shall fall from heaven, and the powers of the heavens
shall be shaken."[28]

The meaning, Bahá'u'lláh explained, is clear. The "moons"
are those religious leaders who take their light from the "Sun"
of Christ. Such "moons" and "stars" fade away each morning
when the Sun of a new day dawns. In like manner, when the
"Sun" of Christ returns, the Sun of the past day is "darkened."
If the "moon" refuses the Light of the new Sun, it too is "darkened" and sheds no light on the problems of men.[29]

This was the meaning of Bahá'u'lláh's words when He entreated such religious leaders not to turn away from Him: "Ye are the stars of the heaven of My knowledge. My mercy desireth not that ye should fall upon the earth."[30]

One more task remained to the itinerant and record-breaking Pope Paul VI. He visited the World Council of Churches in Switzerland in June 1969, thus bringing together leaders from both the Catholic and Protestant faiths. That visit took place one hundred years after Bahá'u'lláh had urged the pope in Rome to do precisely that: to offer His teachings to the other religious leaders of humankind.

First "drink" of the words yourself, Bahá'u'lláh had instructed Pius IX, then "proffer" them to the "peoples of all faiths."

The World Council of Protestant Churches had met before. During one of their international gatherings, the press reported that the delegates found it impossible to reach a vote on the subject of Christ's return. Delegates from 163 denominations from 48 countries "disagreed sharply and fundamentally" on the question of "whether the Christian hope for the establishment of God's kingdom can be fulfilled in this world or only after the second coming of Christ."[31]

He had come, and He had gone!

For sixteen decades, the Báb, Bahá'u'lláh, 'Abdu'l-Bahá, and the followers of Bahá'u'lláh in all parts of the planet, have been telling the Christian world that Christ has already returned. He has come and He has gone, just as He said in the Bible that He would. Christ cautioned that although "all eyes shall see His glory," He would come "as a thief in the night."[32] The parable He told made it clear that the divine "thief" would have come and gone! It happened over a hundred years ago! And that is why a world body of the Christian faith spent hours debating whether they could establish Christ's Kingdom now or only after He returned. That is why a Catholic pope broke all precedents and went to meet with them.

Tragically, they had nothing to say to one another when they met. The pope did not, in fact, understand the impulse that had sent him there. And he demonstrated no awareness of the one message that could have had any relevance for his audience.

And so they all went home.

Ye shut up the kingdom of heaven against men.

Blind Leaders

Bahá'u'lláh has written thus of the clergy of His time: "When We observed carefully, We discovered that Our enemies are, for the most part, the divines."[33]

He addressed them directly, "How long will ye . . . level the spears of hatred at the face of Bahá? . . . follow not your desires which have altered the face of creation."[34]

Bahá'u'lláh tried to open their eyes and ears so they might hear that "new song" spoken of by Isaiah. He said, "Purify your ears that they may hearken unto the Voice of God. . . . Can any one of you race with the Divine Youth in the arena of wisdom and utterance, or soar with Him in the heaven of inner meaning and explanation? . . . Can the one possessed of wooden legs resist him whose feet God hath made of steel? Nay, by Him Who illumineth the whole of creation!"[35]

Bahá'u'lláh offered an ocean of proof to the religious leaders of all Faiths that He was the One they awaited. Yet many not only rejected Bahá'u'lláh, but they actively opposed, persecuted, and tried to stamp out both Bahá'u'lláh and His teachings.

Almost without exception, religious leaders have taken the lead in holding shut the door whenever their followers became interested in the Message of Bahá'u'lláh.

Their attacks on the Revelation and their willingness to re-tell slanders passed on to them by Muslim clergy carry discouraging echoes of similar actions in the early days of Christianity by the same sort of religious opponents.

No wonder Bahá'u'lláh was to write to such clergymen: "O ye that are foolish yet have a name to be wise! Wherefore do ye wear the guise of the shepherd, when inwardly ye have become wolves, intent upon my flock?"[36]

It is also not surprising that Christ Himself would warn against such unseeing shepherds of His flock. Jesus said, "Let them alone: they be blind leaders of the blind. And if the blind lead the blind both shall fall into the ditch."[37]

Yet Bahá'u'lláh in no way sought to degrade or belittle the importance of the world's religious leaders. Rather, He praised unreservedly those religious leaders whose actions and conduct conform to their words. He has said that "The guidance of men hath, at all times, been and is dependent upon these blessed souls."[38]

Of such a sincere religious leader, whatever his religion or denomination, Bahá'u'lláh has also written, "The inmates of Paradise, and the dwellers of the sacred Folds, bless him at eventide and at dawn."[39]

Such spiritual giants, whether Christian, Jewish, Muslim, or of any other religion, are "as the spirit to the body of the world," Bahá'u'lláh declares, and "as an eye unto the world."[40]

It was two Christian clergymen from the missionary field who first introduced the Bahá'í Faith to America in 1893 at the World Parliament of Religions. One wrote a paper describing the "Christ-like" sentiments of Bahá'u'lláh, the other read the document to the assembled audience.

Over four hundred outstanding clergy of the Muslim Faith, some of them the most illustrious in the land, recognized and accepted the Báb and Bahá'u'lláh as the promised Messengers of God. They made great sacrifices for their Faith. Many were killed for their beliefs.

Clergy of all Faiths have since embraced the teachings of Bahá'u'lláh, from Catholic priests to Buddhist monks. But in almost every instance they have been shunned by their former colleagues, belittled, ridiculed, persecuted, and in some instances killed.

It is too late to patch up and sew together a pathetically fragmented Christianity. Hundreds and hundreds of sects in a patchwork quilt of curious variations compete with each other for the Body of Christ. Even the hopeful signs of an ecumenical drawing together is but the unwitting result of Bahá'u'lláh's Message of oneness. Almost against their will the unifying forces of life drive these broken and tattered pieces before the wind toward one common destination—unity.

And if *all* the multitude of Christian sects were to unite, there would still remain Jews, Muslims, Buddhists, Hindus, Zoroastrians, agnostics, atheists, and primitive peoples. Bahá'u'lláh is reaching out an embrace to all religions and all peoples, not just to Christianity alone.

Bahá'u'lláh was saddened at the apathy of the Christian masses who had been given so many opportunities, yet who stood by indifferently while multitudes from other religious heritages entered the Faith of God ahead of them: "O people of the Gospel! They who were not in the Kingdom have now entered it, whilst We behold you, in this day, tarrying at the gate. . . . Open the doors of your hearts. . . . Will ye bar the doors of your houses in My face?"[41]

In a poetic reference to His own appearance as foretold in Christian scripture and to His exile to the land of Jesus, where His Kingdom was established, He asks, "O Bethlehem! This Light hath risen in the orient, and traveled towards the occident, until it reached thee in the evening of its life. Tell Me then: Do the sons recognize the Father, and acknowledge Him, or do they deny Him, even as the people aforetime denied Him [Jesus]?"[42]

———— ❦ ————

15 ❧ THE HEART OF THE WORLD AFIRE

A Spiritual Revolution

Nearly 150 years ago, Bahá'u'lláh warned that a spiritual revolution would invade in every land every institution of the human social order. However painful the process, He warned against efforts to defend standards and institutions that, by their very existence, keep people from becoming aware of the need for a new social order based on the Revelation of God.

The principles of the Bahá'í community are plain:

> If long-cherished ideals and time-honored institutions, if certain social assumptions and religious formulae have ceased to promote the welfare of the generality of mankind, if they no longer minister to the needs of a continually evolving humanity, let them be swept away and relegated to the limbo of obsolescent and forgotten doctrines. Why should these, in a world subject to the immutable law of change and decay, be exempt from the deterioration that must needs overtake every human institution? For legal standards, political and economic theories are solely designed to safeguard the interests of humanity as a whole, and not humanity to be crucified for the preservation of the integrity of any particular law or doctrine.[1]

The truth is, entire civilizations perpetuate themselves long after the Spirit that gave them birth and relevance has departed. We are asking of our present-day civilizations, both East and

West, the vitality, enthusiasm, purity, uprightness and courage of their youth while they are suffering from the diseases of old age. Hardening of the spiritual arteries has set in. Traditional religion in each case has dug down deep into its barrel of spiritual resources and has come up empty.

Both religious and government leaders continue to make adjustments in the old institutions to try and make them relevant. These leaders are confident that the problems are only temporary. They are sure they will find a solution to these passing crises if their people are only patient enough.

The representatives of the established order seem somehow incapable of accepting that we cannot go back to the past or try to solve problems only on a local or national level. Any solution to the crying needs of humanity that is not *planetary* in its scope is doomed to failure. Sectarian religion similarly has no relevance in an age where unity is essential for survival. It is no longer possible to launch our rockets on the oats we feed our horses. A world society is erupting beneath our feet and shaking down the cultural walls behind which we still try to hide.

The world is not suffering from a "temporary maladjustment" in its life. It is suffering from the "death-pangs" of an old, effete, worn-out order. We have become a profit-making world instead of a welfare-producing world. We have become oblivion-seeking people instead of a truth-seeking people.

The tremendous resources of our planet are largely expended on weapons of war and defense, not on health, education, and the elimination of poverty.

How is it possible for any people to turn for guidance concerning peace and welfare to agencies that have been developed for the ends of war and destruction?

Bahá'ís see the current social breakdown as an irresistible natural process. It could have been prevented, and the transition could have been made peaceful and productive if only the leaders of nations had turned to the source of all civilization. Since they did not, the revolt is sweeping away the good with the bad. It seems too difficult and painful to weed out the good trees from the forest of diseased ones. So let it all fall together.

Yet Bahá'ís are firmly obedient to the governments of the nations in which they reside. Bahá'u'lláh Himself commanded them to behave "with loyalty, honesty and truthfulness" to the governments of their countries.[2] The teachings of Bahá'u'lláh's Faith demand not only that the Bahá'ís be loyal to their government, but also forbid any involvement in any political movement, apart from the individual's right to decide his vote in the privacy of his own conscience. Bahá'ís everywhere have a "sacred obligation to promote, in the most effective manner, the best interests of their government and people,"[3] without associating themselves with the diplomatic policies or pursuits of any government. True patriotism, they believe, need not conflict with a person's supreme loyalty to God and to the welfare of the one human race.

Within this clear and undeviating framework, the Bahá'ís of the world labor energetically to change those things that are wrong and unjust. They use all the channels that are open to them. Above all, however, they seek to change hearts, for until we have a new world conscience we cannot have a new world society.

The writings of Bahá'u'lláh's Faith say that the "most vital duty" given to every Bahá'í is to "purify" his character.[4] Every

Bahá'í is commanded to conduct himself in such a manner that he will stand out amongst the people of the world because of his moral qualities. These seemingly impossible goals are within the individual's reach for only one reason. Bahá'u'lláh has created, and God sustains, a true community, a society fit for human beings to live in.

In this day, Bahá'u'lláh says, God loves and aids "those who work in His path in groups."[5] Like a healthy body, the community of Bahá'u'lláh provides the spiritual nourishment that each individual, as a cell in an organism, requires. There is no other way to live.

Far from being negative, the Bahá'í community realizes that the painful ills now afflicting present-day society are the "death pangs" of a dying civilization. They are being accompanied by the "birth pangs" of a new civilization, which is the organic world community, the "Ark of human salvation" now rising in strength and beauty upon the ruins of the old.[6]

Increasingly, it is young people who seem most able to grasp the necessity for this change. Ironically, it is this element of society, regarded as most irresponsible and violent, which best understands that humankind's urgent need is for moral and spiritual regeneration.

*They will experience an emotion
they are not likely to forget.*

Rebels of God

Bahá'u'lláh's community has been driven by youthful energy and zeal since its earliest days. The Herald of the Bahá'í Faith, the Báb, was but twenty-five when His mission began. He was only thirty when an execution squad of 750 soldiers leveled their rifles at Him. The companion who died with Him on that occasion, head upon His breast, was only eighteen.

The overwhelming majority of the Báb's chief disciples were young. The first was twenty-seven, the last nineteen. Behind the dramatic dialogue between the Messenger of God and the kings of the world, hundreds of youths of both sexes willingly laid down their lives for the redemption of mankind. That is how the Revelation was born.

In one inspiring encounter, a handful of young men, 313 in number, "unequipped yet God-intoxicated students, mostly sedentary recluses of the college and cloister" suddenly found themselves "pitted in self-defense against a trained army, well equipped, supported by the masses of the people, blessed by the clergy, headed by a prince of the royal blood" and backed "by the resources of the state."[7]

These early idealistic followers of the Báb rose up as one soul against the corruption and hypocrisy of their society. Their spiritual rebellion against injustices became the "seed" which already is beginning to yield its fruit in the shape of a world-encircling Order whose purpose is to assure the welfare and identity of every human being.

It was no small thing. The French author Renan, in *Les Apôtres*, described one of the dramatic episodes in the rise of the Bahá'í Faith as "a day without parallel perhaps in the history of the world."[8]

Over twenty thousand followers were killed in Persia alone. More of these early believers were slain in one year than there were Christians martyred by official Roman decree in the most terrible eight-year-long persecution by the Emperor Diocletian.

Lord Curzon of Kedleston wrote, "Of no small account, then, must be the tenets of a creed that can awaken in its followers so rare and beautiful a spirit of self-sacrifice."[9]

The spirit that animated and inspired these youthful defenders of the Bahá'í Faith was so moving that Professor E. G. Browne of Cambridge University said, "it can hardly fail to affect most powerfully all subjected to its influence." "Should that spirit once reveal itself to them," he added, "they will experience an emotion which they are not likely to forget."[10]

Bahá'u'lláh Himself was but twenty-seven when He first began teaching in His native province and thirty-six when His ministry began.

'Abdu'l-Bahá was nine when He first understood the great station of His father. He was a small child when He saw Bahá'u'lláh beset with pain and suffering under the iron-yoke of chains in the Black Pit prison. He was nineteen when He left Iraq in exile with His father. He was only twenty-four when He arrived at the prison-city of 'Akká and Bahá'u'lláh turned over to Him the responsibility of dealing with the outside world. He was still young when Bahá'u'lláh passed away and the weight of the entire Bahá'í world fell upon His shoulders.

'Abdu'l-Bahá's youngest brother, Mírzá Mihdí, was but twenty-two when he sacrificed his life in the prison of 'Akká so that the gates of the prison might open and the Spirit of Bahá'u'lláh's Revelation touch the hearts of all mankind.

Shoghi Effendi, 'Abdu'l-Bahá's grandson, was only twenty-five when he was appointed as the Guardian of the Faith and assumed leadership of the global community.

The messenger who carried Bahá'u'lláh's powerful letter to Náṣiri'd-Dín Sháh was scarcely more than a boy, only seventeen. His family despaired of his conduct. They considered him to be what many people today would probably call a delinquent.

Yet he was chosen by Bahá'u'lláh over a crowd of volunteers for this great mission. Alone, and on foot, he walked the entire distance from the prison on the Mediterranean Sea to Ṭihrán, the capital of Persia, a journey of four months.

His name was Áqá Buzurg. He was known as Badí' (which means "wonderful"). He delivered the letter to Náṣiri'd-Dín Sháh, was arrested, and branded and tortured for three successive days. And finally he was beaten to death, and his body was thrown into a pit.

Bahá'u'lláh Himself declared that "the spirit of might and power was breathed" into that youth. He praised Badí' for three years in His writings, saying that his example was as "salt" in the spiritual food needed by humanity.[11]

All over the world, in Africa, Asia, Australia, the islands of the South Pacific, Latin America, North America, and Europe, the number of young people embracing the Faith of Bahá'u'lláh increases each year. Those in their teens and twenties make up the majority of the new "recruits" for Bahá'u'lláh's spiritual army.

In the Bahá'í community there is no generation gap any more than there is a distinction between races or classes. The tragic lack of communication that causes the rift in our sick society need not exist if each individual is accepted on his own merits without regard to age or race, sex or culture. A disciple of the Báb, a youth of nineteen, who was the first to suffer persecution on Persian soil, was accompanied through every humiliation by an elderly man who miraculously withstood one thousand lashes on his back. They suffered together, fellow believers, side by side. It is the same the world over.

Youth is not mainly a time of life, but a state of mind. Years can wrinkle the skin, but losses of ideals can wrinkle the soul and wither the spirit of man, whatever his age—young or old.

------- ❦ -------

The hour of final victory

A World Community

Bahá'u'lláh did not come to any one group of people. He came to the entire world. His Faith calls upon "young and old alike" to make the teaching of His healing, world-redeeming Faith the dominating passion of their lives. Bahá'u'lláh offers a challenge that is today testing the determination, stamina, selflessness, sacrifice, and devotion of people of every race, culture, nation, and position in life. The following words are those of Bahá'u'lláh's great-grandson, Shoghi Effendi, the Bahá'í Faith's appointed Guardian, who inspired and led the worldwide spread of the Message of God:

Under whatever conditions, the dearly loved, the divinely sustained, the onward marching legions of the army of Bahá'u'lláh may be laboring, in whatever theater they may

operate, in whatever climes they may struggle, whether in
the cold and inhospitable territories beyond the Arctic Circle,
or in the torrid zones of both the Eastern and Western Hemi-
spheres; on the borders of the jungles of Burma, Malaya and
India; on the fringes of the deserts of Africa and of the Arabian Peninsula; in the lonely, far-away, backward and sparsely
populated islands dotting the Atlantic, the Pacific and the
Indian Oceans and the North Sea; amidst the diversified tribes
of the Negroes of Africa, the Eskimos and the Lapps of the
Arctic regions, the Mongolians of East and South East Asia,
the Polynesians of the South Pacific Islands, the reservations
of the Red Indians in both American continents, the Maoris
of New Zealand, and the aborigines of Australia; within the
time-honored strongholds of both Christianity and Islám,
whether it be in Mecca, Rome, Cairo, Najaf or Karbilá; or in
towns and cities whose inhabitants are either immersed in
crass materialism, or breathe the fetid air of an aggressive
racialism, or find themselves bound by the chains and fetters
of a haughty intellectualism, or have fallen a prey to the forces
of a blind and militant nationalism, or are steeped in the
atmosphere of a narrow and intolerant ecclesiasticism—to
them all, as well as to those who, as the fortunes of this fate-
laden Crusade prosper, will be called upon to unfurl the standard of an all-conquering Faith in the strongholds of Hinduism, and assist in the breaking up of a rigid age-long caste
system, who will replace the seminaries and monasteries acting as the nurseries of the Buddhist Faith with the divinely-
ordained institutions of Bahá'u'lláh's victorious Order, who
will penetrate the jungles of the Amazon, scale the moun-
tain-fastnesses of Tibet, establish direct contact with the teem-
ing and hapless multitudes in the interior of China, Mongolia

and Japan, sit with the leprous, consort with the outcasts in their penal colonies, traverse the steppes of Russia or scatter throughout the wastes of Siberia, I direct my impassioned appeal to obey, as befits His warriors, the summons of the Lord of Hosts, and prepare for that Day of Days when His victorious battalions will . . . celebrate the hour of final victory.[12]

Peoples of all ages, by the hundreds and by the thousands, from all races and nations, are answering that call.

"The Word of God," Bahá'u'lláh has said, "has set the heart of the world afire. How regrettable if you fail to be enkindled with its flame!"[13]

———— ❦ ————

APPENDIX

Have the stars fallen? Say: *Yea, when He Who is the Self-Subsisting dwelt in the Land of Mystery. Take heed, ye who are endued with discernment! All the signs appeared when We drew forth the Hand of Power from the bosom of majesty and might.*

The Prisoner and the Kings has told of the sad but inevitable fate of those in supreme temporal authority who failed to heed the call of Him Who was the embodiment of all authority, the Manifestation of God, Bahá'u'lláh. So drunk were these rulers with pride and vainglory that they had stopped their ears to any call but self-interest and self-aggrandizement. Hence when the call came to each of them to bow their knee before God's Vicegerent upon earth they had no capacity to hear it. Grave indeed were the consequences, not just for them, as you have read, but also for all humankind.

Bahá'u'lláh clearly stated that had the kings responded to His Message, the Most Great Peace could have been established in His lifetime, for He would be on earth to counsel them. Alas, they did not respond, and so He warned them: "If ye pay no heed unto the counsels which, in peerless and unequivocal language, We have revealed in this Tablet, Divine chastisement shall assail you from every direction, and the sentence of His justice shall be pronounced against you. On that day ye shall have no power to resist Him, and shall recognize your own impotence."[1] When they still did not hearken to His Message, He stated in terse and unequivocal language: "From two ranks amongst men power hath been seized: kings and ecclesiastics."[2] From that moment the downfall of the mightiest potentates in the world proceeded with a speed astonishing to all. And none knew why. This is spiritual history that still needs to be written in detail.

The process did not end with those to whom Bahá'u'lláh addressed specific messages. Governments all over the world have been thrown into confusion and consternation, unable to resolve internal problems, unwilling, for the most part, to unite in a common effort to establish peace and prosperity for all. They are both visionless and impotent to deal with the problems of the world. The root of the world's unrest was accurately described by Shoghi Effendi, Guardian of the Faith, in the early days of the world's Great Depression:

> Is it not a fact—and this is the central idea I desire to emphasize—that the fundamental cause of this world unrest is attributable, not so much to the consequences of what must sooner or later come to be regarded as a transitory dislocation in the affairs of a continually changing world, but rather to the failure of those into whose hands the immediate destinies of peoples and nations have been committed, to adjust their system of economic and political institutions to the imperative needs of a rapidly evolving age? Are not these intermittent crises that convulse present-day society due primarily to the lamentable inability of the world's recognized leaders to read aright the signs of the times, to rid themselves once for all of their preconceived ideas and fettering creeds, and to reshape the machinery of their respective governments according to those standards that are implicit in Bahá'u'lláh's supreme declaration of the Oneness of Mankind—the chief and distinguishing feature of the Faith He proclaimed? For the principle of the Oneness of Mankind, the cornerstone of

Bahá'u'lláh's world-embracing dominion, implies nothing more nor less than the enforcement of His scheme for the unification of the world—the scheme to which we have already referred. "In every Dispensation," writes 'Abdu'l-Bahá, "the light of Divine Guidance has been focussed upon one central theme. . . . In this wondrous Revelation, this glorious century, the foundation of the Faith of God and the distinguishing feature of His Law is the consciousness of the Oneness of Mankind."[3]

However, there have been two monarchs who did read aright the signs of the times and responded to the message of Bahá'u'lláh. The first, Dowager Queen Marie of Romania,[4] early in this century, and the second, His Highness Malietoa Tanumafili II of Samoa, in 1968. His Highness is the first reigning monarch to embrace the Faith of Bahá'u'lláh. About such noble souls Bahá'u'lláh has said,

How great the blessedness that awaiteth the king who will arise to aid My Cause in My Kingdom, who will detach himself from all else but Me! Such a king is numbered with the companions of the Crimson Ark—the Ark which God hath prepared for the people of Bahá. All must glorify his name, must reverence his station, and aid him to unlock the cities with the keys of My Name, the omnipotent Protector of all that inhabit the visible and invisible kingdoms. Such a king is the very eye of mankind, the luminous ornament on the brow of creation, the fountain-head of blessings unto the whole world. Offer up, O people of Bahá, your substance, nay your very lives, for his assistance.[5]

As Bahá'u'lláh clearly states, the Bahá'ís owe such rulers their wholehearted aid and support, even their lives. To them is due our praise and our reverence. We feel, then, a responsibility to bring to the readers of *The Prisoner and the Kings* some tribute to these magnificent souls to round out the story. But far be it from us to venture this. Rather, we have decided to excerpt tributes from the Guardian about Queen Marie and the salient facts that led to her conversion and public statements about the Faith. About His Highness Malietoa Tanumafili II, we have reprinted the article from *The Bahá'í World*, volume 15, which includes his personal letter avowing his belief in Baha'u'llah, as well as the announcement to the Bahá'í world of his declaration as a Bahá'í.

Let us also say in passing that the author of this book, Hand of the Cause of God William Sears, met the Malietoa and they became friends.

Queen Marie of Romania

Who is the sovereign, excepting a single woman, shining in solitary glory, who has, in however small a measure, felt impelled to respond to the poignant call of Bahá'u'lláh? Who amongst the great ones of the earth was inclined to extend this infant Faith of God the benefit of his recognition or support?[6]

Eldest daughter of the Duke of Edinburgh, who was the second son of that Queen to whom Bahá'u'lláh had, in a significant Tablet, addressed words of commendation;

granddaughter of Czar Alexander II to whom an Epistle had been revealed by that same Pen; related by both birth and marriage to Europe's most prominent families; born in the Anglican Faith; closely associated through her marriage with the Greek Orthodox Church, the state religion of her adopted country; herself an accomplished authoress; possessed of a charming and radiant personality; highly talented, clear-visioned, daring and ardent by nature; keenly devoted to all enterprises of a humanitarian character, she, alone among her sister-queens, alone among all those of royal birth or station, was moved to spontaneously acclaim the greatness of the Message of Bahá'u'lláh, to proclaim His Fatherhood, as well as the Prophethood of Muḥammad, to commend the Bahá'í teachings to all men and women, and to extol their potency, sublimity and beauty.

Through the fearless acknowledgment of her belief to her own kith and kin, and particularly to her youngest daughter; through three successive encomiums that constitute her greatest and abiding legacy to posterity; through three additional appreciations penned by her as her contribution to Bahá'í publications; through several letters written to friends and associates, as well as those addressed to her guide and spiritual mother; through various tokens expressive of faith and gratitude for the glad-tidings that had been brought to her through the orders for Bahá'í books placed by her and her youngest daughter; and lastly through her frustrated pilgrimage to the Holy Land for the express purpose of paying homage at the graves of the Founders of the Faith—through such acts as these this illustrious queen may well deserve to rank as the first of those royal supporters of the Cause of God who are to arise in the future, and each of whom, in the words of Bahá'u'lláh Himself, is to be acclaimed as "the very eye of mankind, the luminous ornament on the brow of creation, the fountainhead of blessings unto the whole world."

"Some of those of my caste," she, in a personal letter, has significantly testified, "wonder at and disapprove my courage to step forward pronouncing words not habitual for crowned heads to pronounce, but I advance by an inner urge I cannot resist. With bowed head I recognize that I too am but an instrument in greater Hands, and I rejoice in the knowledge."

A note which Martha Root, upon her arrival in Bucharest, sent to her Majesty and a copy of *Bahá'u'lláh and the New Era,* which accompanied the note, and which so absorbed the Queen's attention that she continued reading it into the small hours of the morning, led, two days later, to the Queen's granting Martha Root an audience, on January 30, 1926, in Controceni Palace in Bucharest, in the course of which her Majesty avowed her belief that "these teachings are the solution for the world's problems"; and from these followed her publication, that same year on her own initiative, of those three epoch-making testimonies which appeared in nearly two hundred newspapers of the United States and Canada, and which were subsequently translated and published in Europe, China, Japan, Australia, the Near East and the Islands of the seas.

In the first of these testimonies she affirmed that the writings of Bahá'u'lláh and 'Abdu'l-Bahá are "a great cry toward peace, reaching beyond all limits of frontiers, above all dissensions about rites and dogmas. . . . It is a wondrous message that Bahá'u'lláh and His Son 'Abdu'l-Bahá have given us! They have not set it up aggressively, knowing that the germ of eternal truth which lies at its core cannot but take root and spread . . . It is Christ's message taken up anew, in the same words almost, but adapted to the thousand years and more difference that lies between the year one and to-day." She added a remarkable admonition, reminiscent of the telling words of Dr. Benjamin Jowett, who had hailed the Faith, in his conversation with his pupil, Prof. Lewis Campbell, as "the greatest light that has come into the world since the time of Jesus Christ," and cautioned him to "watch it" and never let it out of his sight. "If ever," wrote the Queen, "the name of Bahá'u'lláh or 'Abdu'l-Bahá comes to your attention, do not put their writings from you. Search out their books, and let their glorious, peace-bringing, love-creating words and lessons sink into your hearts as they have into mine. . . . Seek them and be the happier."

In another of these testimonies, wherein she makes a significant comment on the station of the Arabian Prophet, she declared: "God is all. Everything. He is the power behind all beings. . . . His is the voice within us that shows us good and evil. But mostly we ignore or misunderstand this voice. Therefore, did He choose His Elect to come down amongst us upon earth to make clear His Word, His real meaning. Therefore the Prophets; therefore Christ, Muḥammad, Bahá'u'lláh, for man needs from time to time a voice upon earth to bring God to him, to sharpen the realization of the existence of the true God. Those voices sent to us had to become flesh, so that with our earthly ears we should be able to hear and understand."

In appreciation of these testimonies a communication was addressed to her, in the name of the followers of

Bahá'u'lláh in East and West, and in the course of the deeply touching letter which she sent in reply she wrote: "Indeed a great light came to me with the Message of Bahá'u'lláh and 'Abdu'l-Bahá. . . . My youngest daughter finds also great strength and comfort in the teachings of the beloved Masters. We pass on the Message from mouth to mouth, and all those we give it to see a light suddenly lighting before them, and much that was obscure and perplexing becomes simple, luminous and full of hope as never before. That my open letter was a balm to those suffering for the Cause, is indeed a great happiness to me, and I take it as a sign that God accepted my humble tribute. The occasion given me to be able to express myself publicly was also His work, for indeed it was a chain of circumstances of which each link led me unwittingly one step further, till suddenly all was clear before my eyes and I understood why it had been. Thus does He lead us finally to our ultimate destiny. . . . Little by little the veil is lifting, grief tore it in two. And grief was also a step leading me ever nearer truth; therefore do I not cry out against grief!"

In a significant and moving letter to an intimate American friend of hers, residing in Paris, she wrote: "Lately a great hope has come to me from one 'Abdu'l-Bahá. I have found in His and His Father, Bahá'u'lláh's Message of faith, all my yearning for real religion satisfied. . . . I mean: these Books have strengthened me beyond belief, and I am now ready to die any day full of hope. But I pray God not to take me away yet, for I still have a lot of work to do."

And again in one of her later appreciations of the Faith: "The Bahá'í teaching brings peace and understanding. It is like a wide embrace gathering all those who have long searched for words of hope. . . . Saddened by the continual strife amongst believers of many confessions and wearied of their intolerance towards each other, I discovered in the Bahá'í teaching the real spirit of Christ so often denied and misunderstood." And again, this wonderful confession: "The Bahá'í teaching brings peace to the soul and hope to the heart. To those in search of assurance the words of the Father are as a fountain in the desert after long wandering."

"The beautiful truth of Bahá'u'lláh," she wrote to Martha Root, "is with me always, a help and an inspiration. What I wrote was because my heart overflowed with gratitude for the reflection you brought me. I am happy if you think I helped. I thought it might bring truth nearer because my words are read by so many."

In the course of a visit to the Near East she expressed her intention of visiting the Bahá'í Shrines, and, accompanied by her youngest daughter, actually passed through Haifa, and was within sight of her goal, when she was denied the right to make the pilgrimage she had planned—to the keen disappointment of the aged Greatest Holy Leaf who had eagerly expected her arrival. A few months later, in June, 1931, she wrote in the course of a letter to Martha Root: "Both Ileana and I were cruelly disappointed at having been prevented going to the holy Shrines. . . . but at that time we were going through a cruel crisis, and every movement I made was being turned against me and being politically exploited in an unkind way. It caused me a good deal of suffering and curtailed my liberty most unkindly. . . . But the beauty of truth remains, and I cling to it through all the vicissitudes of a life become rather sad. . . . I am glad to hear that your traveling has been so fruitful, and I wish you continual success knowing what a beautiful Message you are carrying from land to land."

After this sad disappointment she wrote to a friend of her childhood who dwelt near 'Akká, in a house formerly occupied by Bahá'u'lláh: "It was indeed nice to hear from you, and to think that you are of all things living near Haifa and are, as I am, a follower of the Bahá'í teachings. It interests me that you are living in that special house . . . I was so intensely interested and studied each photo intently. It must be a lovely place . . . and the house you live in, so incredibly attractive and made precious by its associations with the Man we all venerate."

Her last public tribute to the Faith she had dearly loved was made two years before her death. "More than ever today," she wrote, "when the world is facing such a crisis of bewilderment and unrest, must we stand firm in Faith seeking that which binds together instead of tearing asunder. To those searching for light, the Bahá'í teachings offer a star which will lead them to deeper understanding, to assurance, peace and goodwill with all men."

Martha Root's own illuminating record is given in one of her articles as follows: "For ten years Her Majesty and her daughter, HRH Princess Ileana (now Arch-Duchess Anton) have read with interest each new book about the Bahá'í Movement, as soon as it came from the press Received in audience by Her Majesty in Pelisor Palace, Sinaia, in 1927, after the passing of His Majesty King Ferdinand, her husband, she graciously gave me an interview, speaking of the Bahá'í teachings about immortality. She had on her table and on the divan a number of Bahá'í books, for she had just been reading in each of them the Teachings about life after death. She asked the writer to give her greeting to . . . the friends in Iran and to the many American Bahá'ís, who she said had been so remarkably kind to her during her trip through the United States the year before. . . . Meeting the Queen again on January 19, 1928, in the Royal Palace in Belgrade, where she and HRH Princess Ileana were guests of the Queen of Yugoslavia—and they had brought some of their Bahá'í books with them—the words that I shall remember longest of all that her dear Majesty said were these: 'The ultimate dream which we shall realize is that the Bahá'í channel of thought has such strength, it will serve little by little to become a light to all those searching for the real expression of Truth.' . . . Then in the audience in Controceni Palace, on February 16, 1934, when her Majesty was told that the Rumanian translation of *Bahá'u'lláh and the New Era* had just been published in Bucharest, she said she was so happy that her people were to have the blessing of reading this precious teaching. . . . And now today, February 4, 1936, I have just had another audience with Her Majesty in Controceni Palace, in Bucharest. . . . Again Queen Marie of Rumania received me cordially in her softly lighted library, for the hour was six o'clock. . . . What a memorable visit it was! . . . She also told me that when she was in London she had met a Bahá'í, Lady Blomfield, who had shown her the original Message that Bahá'u'lláh had sent to her grand-mother, Queen Victoria, in London. She asked the writer about the progress of the Bahá'í Movement, especially in the Balkan countries. . . . She spoke too of several Bahá'í books, the depths of Íqán,* and especially of *Gleanings from the Writings of Bahá'u'lláh,* which she said was a wonderful book! To quote her own words: 'Even doubters would find a powerful strength in it, if they would read it alone, and would give their souls time to expand.' ... I asked her if I could perhaps speak of the brooch which historically is precious to Bahá'ís, and she replied, 'Yes, you may.' Once, and it was in 1928, Her dear Majesty had given the writer a gift, a lovely and rare brooch which had been a gift to the Queen from her royal relatives in Russia some years ago. It was two little wings of wrought gold and silver, set with tiny diamond chips, and joined together with one large pearl. 'Always you are giving gifts to others, and I am going to give you a gift from me,' said the Queen smiling, and she herself clasped it onto my dress. The wings and the pearl made it seem 'Light-bearing' Bahá'í! It was sent the same week to Chicago as a gift to the Bahá'í Temple ... and at the National Bahá'í Convention which was in session that spring, a demur was made—should a gift from the Queen be sold? Should it not be kept as a souvenir of the first Queen who arose to promote the Faith of Bahá'u'lláh? However, it was sold immediately and the money given to the Temple, for all Bahá'ís were giving to the utmost to forward this mighty structure, the first of its kind in the United States of America. Mr. Willard Hatch, a Bahá'í of Los Angeles, Calif., who bought the exquisite brooch, took it to Haifa, Palestine, in 1931, and placed it in the Archives on Mt. Carmel, where down the ages it will rest with the Bahá'í treasures."

---

* The Kitáb-i-Íqán, the foremost doctrinal work of Bahá'u'lláh.

In July, 1938, Queen Marie of Rumania passed away. A message of condolence was communicated, in the name of all Bahá'í communities in East and West, to her daughter, the Queen of Yugoslavia, to which she replied expressing "sincere thanks to all of Bahá'u'lláh's followers." The National Spiritual Assembly of the Bahá'ís of Persia addressed, on behalf of the followers of the Faith in Bahá'u'lláh's native land, a letter expressive of grief and sympathy to her son, the King of Rumania and the Rumanian Royal Family, the text of which was in both Persian and English. An expression of profound and loving sympathy was sent by Martha Root to Princess Ileana, and was gratefully acknowledged by her. Memorial gatherings were held in the Queen's memory, at which a meed of honor was paid to her bold and epochal confession of faith in the Fatherhood of Bahá'u'lláh, to her recognition of the station of the Prophet of Islám and to the several encomiums from her pen. On the first anniversary of her death the National Spiritual Assembly of the Bahá'ís of the United States and Canada demonstrated its grateful admiration and affection for the deceased Queen by associating itself, through an imposing floral offering, with the impressive memorial service, held in her honor, and arranged by the Rumanian Minister, in Bethlehem Chapel, at the Cathedral of Washington, DC, at which the American delegation, headed by the Secretary of State and including government officials and representatives of the Army and Navy, the British, French and Italian Ambassadors, and representatives of other European embassies and legations joined in a common tribute to one who, apart from the imperishable renown achieved by her in the Kingdom of Bahá'u'lláh, had earned, in this earthly life, the esteem and love of many a soul living beyond the confines of her own country.[7]

His Highness Malietoa Tanumafili, II

The following is from appeared under the title "First Head Of State Embraces The Cause Of Bahá'u'lláh," in *The Bahá'í World,* volume 15, pp. 180–3.

That His Highness Malietoa Tanumafili II, the first reigning monarch to embrace the Cause of Bahá'u'lláh, should do so during the year marking the centenary of the revelation of the *Súriy-i-Mulúk*[8] and that he should openly declare his faith to his fellow believers during the days marking the one hundredth anniversary of the revelation of the *Kitáb-i-Aqdas*[9] must surely be recognized as one of the most significant events in the evolution of the Formative Age. It is also most interesting that his country, Western Samoa, is located in the middle of the vast Pacific Ocean bringing to mind the prophecy of Bahá'u'lláh about His revelation that *should they attempt to conceal its light on the continent, it will assuredly rear its head in the midmost heart of the oceans, and, raising its voice, proclaim: "I am the life-giver of the world!"*[10]

The events leading up to the acceptance of the Faith by His Highness began with the decision of the Universal House of Justice to present a deluxe edition of *The Promulgation of Bahá'u'lláh* to today's reigning monarchs and heads of state. The Malietoa was one of the one hundred and forty-one to receive this book, re-stating Bahá'u'lláh's Own announcement to the kings and rulers of His day.

The Hand of the Cause Dr. Ugo Giachery, who was in Samoa on his return from the Intercontinental Conference in Sydney in October, 1967, was requested by the National

Spiritual Assembly of the Bahá'ís of the South Pacific Ocean to present *The Proclamation of Bahá'u'lláh* to the head of state of Western Samoa, which he was glad to do. An appointment was made, and in the late afternoon of October 27, 1967, His Highness Malietoa Tanumafili received Dr. Giachery and the National Spiritual Assembly representative, Mr. Virgil Wilson, at a newly built Samoan *fale* on a tiny off-shore island at Letulatla Lefata. It was at this spot that His Highness had some years before been invested with the title "Malietoa."

His Highness offered Dr. Giachery his chair and after exchanging courtesies the book was presented on behalf of the Universal House of Justice. The Malietoa was greatly pleased to receive it and thoughtfully leafed through its pages. The Hand of the Cause explained what the volume contained and drew attention to the list of kings and rulers to whom the original Tablets had been addressed. Throughout the conversation which lasted for almost ninety minutes many questions about the Faith were answered and His Highness expressed great interest in the Bahá'í Teachings. As Dr. Giachery prepared to take his leave, the Malietoa grasped his hands and expressed the hope that he would return some time for another visit. No one knew at that time how soon this hope was to be realized.

In early December, 1967, Dr. Giachery reported that he had recently received two letters from the American pioneer, Mr. Virgil Wilson, in which he stated that on more than one occasion the Malietoa had stated his desire to join the Faith. Because of the importance of the possibility that one of so high a rank and occupying a station which had been so greatly exalted by Bahá'u'lláh would embrace the

Cause, the Universal House of Justice asked the Hand of the Cause Dr. Ugo Giachery to return to Western Samoa to discuss this matter with His Highness.

The first historic meeting with the Malietoa took place at his official residence in Vailima on Monday, January 16, 1968. Dr. Giachery reports, "On arrival at the main entrance a triumphal chant was heard and His Highness rushed in person to the automobile with outstretched hands, bidding us welcome. After the exchange of greetings, he led us along the main staircase to the large reception hall where we were seated. . ." During the course of the conversation which followed, the Malietoa declared, "I am a Bahá'í . . . I believe in Bahá'u'lláh."

Afterward the Hand of the Cause cabled the Universal House of Justice:

"HEARTY WELCOME JOYFUL CONVERSATION CONFIRM CONVICTION. . . ."

It is noteworthy that it was this Malietoa's great-great-grandfather, Malietoa Tavita, who accepted Christianity in 1830 in response to the teaching work of John Williams of the London Missionary Society.

On February 11, 1968, another meeting took place at the private residence of the Malietoa. His Highness showed keen interest and asked many questions as Dr. Giachery reviewed with him the principles of the Faith and its administration. Again he stated that he believed in Bahá'u'lláh and His Revelation. Within the hour, Dr. Giachery cabled the Universal House of Justice:

"TODAYS INTERVIEW CONFIRMS HEARTFELT ACCEPTANCE . . ."

Later, on February 19, 1968, the Malietoa wrote the Universal House of Justice expressing appreciation for "the beautiful and precious volume containing some letters addressed by Bahá'u'lláh, the exalted Founder of the Bahá'í Faith, to the rulers of His time . . . ," and added:

"This gift is immensely appreciated because it has assisted me in better understanding . . . the Teachings of Bahá'u'lláh, which I have fully and wholeheartedly accepted. I do consider myself a member of the Bahá'í Faith, even if at this time I do not deem it necessary to make a public declaration, but I do hope that your prayers at the Holy place of our Faith will attract upon me the divine assistance needed to carry on my duties and to increase my spiritual powers which will make of me a just and honored ruler."

The Universal House of Justice replied:

"That the first ruling monarch should declare his whole-hearted acceptance of Bahá'u'lláh during the centenary of Bahá'u'lláh's proclamation brought great happiness to our hearts. Our souls are filled with feelings of awe and wonderment as we contemplate the fulfilment, in this day, of some of the prophecies of Bahá'u'lláh regarding the kings and rulers of the world. . . .

"The historic significance of your membership in the Bahá'í Faith has been recorded in our annals. We fully appreciate your feeling not to make a public declaration at the present time. We shall await word from you before informing the Bahá'ís of the world of this momentous event in the history of our Faith, which will fire their hearts with new zeal and enthusiasm enabling them to rise to new heights of endeavour in their God-given role in the quickening of mankind."

Five years and one month later, His Highness made known to his fellow believers his faith in Bahá'u'lláh.

A transcription of the Malietoa's letter letter is below.

March 31, 1973

Greatly esteemed members of the Universal House of Justice, much admired Hands of the Cause of God, respected Counsellors and honoured delegates attending the Third International Convention

My spiritual Brethren:

It is a joy for me and for my fellow Bahá'ís of the Samoan Islands in the heart of the Pacific, to be with you in spirit and with the friends of the God throughout the world, in celebrating this most significant first century of the revelation of the Kitáb-i-Aqdas, the Most Holy Book of Bahá'u'lláh.

We pray for the success of the historic convention now being held in the shadow of the Mountain of God in the Holy Land. Although we are unable to be with you in person on this memorable occasion, our hearts share with you these never to be forgotten days and the knowledge of the tremendous victories won for the Faith of God.

To the north, to the south, to the east and to the west, to the most populous and to the most remote places, we send our fond greetings and cherished love. May the spirit created by your gathering at the Holy Shrines pave the way for the rapid establishment of the Kingdom of God on earth and the unity of all the peoples of the world.

Alofa tele atu lava matou uma I Samoa nei.[11]

[signed] Malietoa Tanumafili II

Following the Malietoa's letter to the Universal House of Justice, it released the following message to the Bahá'ís of the world:

7 May 1973

To the Bahá'ís of the world

Dear Bahá'í friends,

It is now possible to share with you all the news of an event which crowns the victories with which Bahá'u'lláh has blessed His followers during the Nine Year Plan, an event of which the true significance will be fully understood only in the course of centuries to come: a reigning monarch has accepted the Message of Bahá'u'lláh.

Among those to whom The Proclamation of Bahá'u'lláh was presented in 1967 was His Highness Malietoa Tanumafili II, the Head of State of the independent nation of Western Samoa in the heart of the Pacific Ocean. His Highness, who had already heard of the Faith, showed immediately that the sacred Words had touched his heart, and the Universal House of Justice thereupon asked the Hand of the Cause Dr. Ugo Giachery, who had presented the book to him, to return to Western Samoa for further audiences with His Highness. Following this visit the Malietoa conveyed his acceptance of the Faith of Bahá'u'lláh to the Universal House of Justice and became the first reigning sovereign to enter beneath the shade of this Cause.

In its Riḍván 1967 message the Universal House of Justice announced that it would present to Heads of State around the world a collection of Tablets Bahá'u'lláh addressed to the kings and rulers of the world a century before. His Highness Malietoa Tanumafili II was one of the recipients.

His Highness decided, with the full agreement of the Universal House of Justice, that it was not propitious to make his declaration public at that time. He has been visited from time to time by Hands of the Cause and other believers, and continual touch with His Highness has been maintained by the House of Justice through Mr. Suhayl 'Alá'í, a member of the Continental Board of Counsellors for Australasia. Gradually the Malietoa has let it be known to those around him that he has accepted Bahá'u'lláh. Now he has judged the time ripe to share this wondrous news with his fellow-believers in all parts of the world, by addressing to the International Bahá'í Convention the gracious and inspiring message of which a copy is enclosed with this letter.[12]

> With loving Bahá'í greetings,
> The Universal House of Justice

NOTES

Chapter 2

1. E. G. Browne, quoted in J. E. Esslemont, *Bahá'u'lláh and the New Era,* p. 39.
2. Bahá'u'lláh, Súriy-i-Mulúk, ¶13, in *Summons of the Lord of Hosts.*
3. Bahá'u'lláh, *Epistle to the Son of the Wolf,* p. 57.
4. Nabíl-i-A'zam, *The Dawn-Breakers,* p. 608.
5. Bahá'u'lláh, *Epistle to the Son of the Wolf,* p. 21.
6. Ibid., p. 40.
7. Bahá'u'lláh, Súriy-i-Haykal, ¶230, in *Summons of the Lord of Hosts.*
8. Nabíl-i-A'zam, *The Dawn-Breakers,* pp. 631–2.
9. J. E. Esslemont, *Bahá'u'lláh and the New Era,* p. 59.

Chapter 3

1. Bahá'u'lláh, Súriy-i-Haykal, ¶131, in *Summons of the Lord of Hosts.*
2. Ibid., ¶142.
3. The Kitáb-i-Aqdas, the "Most Holy Book," Bahá'u'lláh's book of laws for the new dispensation and the world commonwealth.
4. Bahá'u'lláh, Súriy-i-Haykal, ¶137, in *Summons of the Lord of Hosts.*
5. Bahá'u'lláh, quoted in *Promised Day Is Come,* ¶123.
6. Bahá'u'lláh, Súriy-i-Haykal, ¶137, in *Summons of the Lord of Hosts.*
7. Ibid., ¶138.
8. Ibid., ¶131–3.
9. C. D. Hazen, *Europe Since 1815,* p. 199.
10. Bahá'u'lláh, Súriy-i-Haykal, ¶138, in *Summons of the Lord of Hosts.*
11. Ibid.
12. 'Abdu'l-Bahá, quoted in *Promised Day Is Come,* ¶225.
13. Bahá'u'lláh, Súriy-i-Mulúk, ¶58, 79, in *Summons of the Lord of Hosts.*
14. Ibid., ¶79.
15. Bahá'u'lláh, Súriy-i-Haykal, ¶138, in ibid.
16. Ibid.
17. Isaiah 24.
18. Bahá'u'lláh, Súriy-i-Haykal, ¶164, in *Summons of the Lord of Hosts.*
19. Isaiah 24:21.

Chapter 4

1. Bahá'u'lláh, Kitáb-i-Aqdas, ¶86.
2. Ibid.
3. Bahá'u'lláh, Hidden Words, Persian, no. 64.
4. Bahá'u'lláh, Kitáb-i-Aqdas, ¶86.

5. Bahá'u'lláh, Súriy-i-Mulúk, ¶15, in *Summons of the Lord of Hosts*.
6. Ibid., ¶8.
7. Ibid.
8. Bahá'u'lláh, *Gleanings*, no. 117.
9. Bahá'u'lláh, Súriy-i-Mulúk, ¶21, in *Summons of the Lord of Hosts*.
10. Bahá'u'lláh, quoted in 'Abdu'l-Bahá, *A Traveller's Narrative*, p. xi.
11. Ibid.
12. Ibid.
13. Bahá'u'lláh, Kitáb-i-Aqdas, ¶90.
14. Ibid.
15. Bahá'u'lláh, Súriy-i-Mulúk, ¶85, in *Summons of the Lord of Hosts*.
16. Ironically, the Hohenzollern Crown Prince, William, served in a Nazi motor division and was captured by the French. The youngest son of Kaiser William II, August Wilhelm, also appeared in the ranks of the Nazis and fell with them.
17. See A. J. P. Taylor, *The Hapsburg Monarchy, 1809–1918*.
18. Jeremiah 49:38.

Chapter 5

1. Bahá'u'lláh, Súriy-i-Haykal, ¶158, in *Summons of the Lord of Hosts*.
2. Ibid., ¶170.
3. Ibid., ¶160.
4. Ibid.
5. Ibid., ¶158.
6. Ibid., ¶162.
7. Ibid., ¶170.
8. Ibid., ¶162.
9. Shoghi Effendi, *Promised Day Is Come*, ¶138.
10. Bahá'u'lláh, Súriy-i-Haykal, ¶178, in *Summons of the Lord of Hosts*.
11. Ibid., ¶158.
12. Haggai 2:7, 22.

Chapter 6

1. Bahá'u'lláh, Kitáb-i-Aqdas, ¶85.
2. Ibid.
3. Bahá'u'lláh, *Gleanings*, no. 118.5.
4. Bahá'u'lláh, *Epistle to the Son of the Wolf*, p. 24.
5. Ibid., p. 27.
6. Bahá'u'lláh, *Gleanings*, no. 163.2.
7. Ibid.
8. Ibid., no. 164.7.

9. Jeremiah 51:20.
10. Bahá'u'lláh, Súriy-i-Mulúk, ¶64, in *Summons of the Lord of Hosts*.
11. Ibid., ¶15.
12. Shoghi Effendi, *Promised Day Is Come*, ¶146.
13. Ibid., ¶147.
14. Zephaniah 1:4–8.

Chapter 7

1. Bahá'u'lláh, Súriy-i-Haykal, ¶171, in *Summons of the Lord of Hosts*.
2. Ibid., ¶172.
3. Ibid., ¶171.
4. Ibid., ¶172.
5. Ibid., ¶173.
6. Ibid., ¶175.
7. Ibid., ¶176.
8. Shoghi Effendi, *Promised Day Is Come*, ¶163.
9. Queen Marie of Romania, quoted in *God Passes By*, p. 391.
10. Ibid.
11. Bahá'u'lláh, Kitáb-i-Aqdas, ¶84.
12. Bahá'u'lláh, quoted in *Promised Day Is Come*, ¶185.
13. Bahá'u'lláh, *Gleanings*, no. 112.
14. Bahá'u'lláh, quoted in *God Passes By*, p. 225.

Chapter 8

1. Bahá'u'lláh, *Epistle to the Son of the Wolf*, p. 11.
2. Quoted in *God Passes By*, p. 79.
3. Mírzá Áqá Khán, quoted in ibid., p. 105.
4. Bahá'u'lláh, quoted in ibid.
5. Ezekiel 8:4.
6. Ezekiel 43:1–2.

Chapter 9

1. Náṣiri'd-Dín Sháh, quoted in Shoghi Effendi, *God Passes By*, p. 225.
2. Bahá'u'lláh, quoted in Shoghi Effendi, *God Passes By*, p. 198.
3. Bahá'u'lláh, Súriy-i-Mulúk, ¶96, in *Summons of the Lord of Hosts*.
4. Isaiah 14:5,27
5. Bahá'u'lláh, Súriy-i-Mulúk, ¶26, in *Summons of the Lord of Hosts*.
6. Bahá'u'lláh, *Gleanings*, no. 112.
7. Daniel 8:23–25.

8. Bahá'u'lláh, Súriy-i-Mulúk, ¶98, in *Summons of the Lord of Hosts*.
9. Ibid., ¶99.
10. Ibid.
11. Shoghi Effendi, *Promised Day Is Come*, ¶171.

Chapter 10

1. John 10:16.
2. The text of this Tablet can be found in *Bahá'í Prayers*, pp. 319–27.
3. Bahá'u'lláh, Kitáb-i-Aqdas, ¶89.
4. Isaiah 41.
5. Micah 7:12.
6. Shamsí Big, quoted in Shoghi Effendi, *God Passes By*, p. 160.
7. Nabíl-i-A'zám, quoted in ibid., p. 161.
8. Bahá'u'lláh, Súriy-i-Haykal, ¶58, 69, 72, 81, in *Summons of the Lord of Hosts*.
9. Bahá'u'lláh, quoted in Shoghi Effendi, *God Passes By*, p. 160.
10. Ibid., pp. 160–61.
11. Shoghi Effendi, *God Passes By*, p. 171
12. Bahá'u'lláh, quoted in ibid.
13. Ibid.
14. Shoghi Effendi, *God Passes By*, p. 171.
15. Bahá'u'lláh, Hidden Words, Persian, no. 54.
16. Ibid., nos. 49, 51.
17. Bahá'u'lláh, Súriy-i-Haykal, ¶178, in *Summons of the Lord of Hosts*.
18. Shoghi Effendi, *God Passes By*, p. 170.
19. Ibid.
20. Ibid., p. 179.
21. Bahá'u'lláh, quoted in Shoghi Effendi, *God Passes By*, p. 184. Author's note: One hundred years later, the author of this book was present at the centenary commemoration of Bahá'u'lláh's arrival in the Holy Land. Already His prophecy had come true. News was being shared from all parts of the earth announcing the entry of great numbers of new Bahá'ís into the Faith of Bahá'u'lláh. They were flocking to His standard in America, Asia, Europe, North and South America, Australia, and in the islands of the Pacific, Atlantic and Indian Oceans, and the Mediterranean and Caribbean Sea. Peoples and races in all nations, especially among the youth of the world, were embracing the Bahá'í Faith in over thirty thousand centers, in almost every section of the world. Indeed, all segments of humanity were now "enlisting" beneath the "banner" of Bahá'u'lláh's Faith.
22. Bahá'u'lláh, quoted in Shoghi Effendi, *God Passes By*, p. 181
23. Bahá'u'lláh, quoted in Shoghi Effendi, *World Order of Bahá'u'lláh*, p. 105
24. Bahá'u'lláh, quoted in Shoghi Effendi, *God Passes By*, p. 181.

25. Áqá Riḍá, quoted in ibid.

26. Bahá'u'lláh, quoted in ibid., p. 182.

27. Shoghi Effendi, *God Passes By,* p. 183.

28. 'Abdu'l-Bahá, *Some Answered Questions,* p. 32.

29. Psalms 2:2–12.

30. Muḥammad, quoted in *Epistle to the Son of the Wolf,* p. 177.

31. Ibid., p. 179.

32. The year 1260 in the Muslim calendar (the one used in both Persia and Turkey) was the year 1844 of the Gregorian calendar. For the many repeated references to the year 1260/1844 from both Christianity and Islam, see William Sears, *Thief in the Night,* pp. 8–28.

33. Islamic hadith, quoted in Shoghi Effendi, *God Passes By,* p. 184.

34. Bahá'u'lláh, *Epistle to the Son of the Wolf,* p. 46

35. See Micah 7. *Thief in the Night* devotes an entire chapter to the incredible story of the fulfillment of these prophecies; see pp. 117–23.

36. Bahá'u'lláh, *Epistle to the Son of the Wolf,* p. 146.

37. Bahá'u'lláh, quoted in Shoghi Effendi, *God Passes By,* p. 187.

38. Ibid., p. 185.

39. Bahá'u'lláh, *Gleanings,* no. 115.6.

40. Shoghi Effendi, *God Passes By,* p. 186.

Chapter 11

1. 'Abdu'l-Bahá, *A Traveller's Narrative,* p. 54.

2. Bahá'u'lláh, Súriy-i-Mulúk, ¶58 in *Summons of the Lord of Hosts.*

3. Ibid., ¶59–60.

4. Ibid., ¶61.

5. Ibid., ¶62–63.

6. Bahá'u'lláh, Suriy-i-Haykal, ¶179, in ibid.

7. Ibid.

8. Ibid.

9. Psalms 136:1, 17, 23, 24.

10. Bahá'u'lláh, Lawḥ-i-Ra'ís, ¶9, in *Summons of the Lord of Hosts.*

11. Bahá'u'lláh, Súriy-i-Mulúk, ¶86 in ibid.

12. Shoghi Effendi, *God Passes By,* p. 158.

13. Bahá'u'lláh, Súriy-i-Mulúk, ¶26 in *Summons of the Lord of Hosts.*

14. Ibid., ¶36.

15. Bahá'u'lláh, Lawḥ-i-Fu'ád, ¶13, in ibid.

16. Bahá'u'lláh, Súriy-i-Ra'ís, ¶5, in ibid.

17. Ibid.

18. Bahá'u'lláh, Lawḥ-i-Ra'ís, ¶7, in ibid.

19. Bahá'u'lláh, Súriy-i-Mulúk, ¶26, in ibid.

20. Ibid., ¶53.
21. Bahá'u'lláh, Kitáb-i-Aqdas, ¶89.
22. Shoghi Effendi, *Promised Day Is Come,* ¶245.

Chapter 12

1. Shoghi Effendi, *God Passes By,* p. 191.
2. E. G. Browne, quoted in H. M. Balyuzi, *Edward Granville Browne and the Bahá'í Faith,* p. 53.
3. Ibid., p. 56.
4. Bahá'u'lláh, quoted in Lady Blomfield, *The Chosen Highway,* p. 64.
5. Psalms 89:3, 27, 28, 37.
6. Isaiah 59:20, 21; 60:1, 2, 3, 12, 16.
7. 'Abdu'l-Bahá, quoted in Shoghi Effendi, *God Passes By,* p. 270.
8. Habakkuk 1:5.
9. Daniel 2:44.
10. 'Abdu'l-Bahá, *Promulgation of Universal Peace,* p. 224.

Chapter 13

1. Bahá'u'lláh, Súrih-i-Mulúk, ¶3, in *Summons of the Lord of Hosts.*
2. Bahá'u'lláh, Kitáb-i-Aqdas, ¶84.
3. Bahá'u'lláh, Súrih-i-Mulúk, ¶20.
4. Bahá'u'lláh, quoted in Shoghi Effendi, *God Passes By,* p. 230; Bahá'u'lláh, *Gleanings,* no. 110; ibid., no. 18.1
5. Jeremiah 25:15, 26–29.
6. See William Sears, *Release the Sun,* pp. 278–79, for an account of this dramatic event, described by the French author A. L. M. Nicholas as something "unique in the annals of the history of humanity."
7. Amos 1:14–15, 8:11.
8. Amos 1:2,
9. Bahá'u'lláh, Súrih-i-Mulúk, ¶12, in *Summons of the Lord of Hosts.*
10. Bahá'u'lláh, quoted in Shoghi Effendi, *God Passes By,* p. 224.
11. Bahá'u'lláh, quoted in Shoghi Effendi, *Promised Day Is Come,* ¶9.
12. Bahá'u'lláh, quoted in Shoghi Effendi, *God Passes By,* p. 220.

Chapter 14

1. Bahá'u'lláh, *Gleanings,* no. 117.
2. Bahá'u'lláh, Súriy-i-Haykal, ¶182, in *Summons of the Lord of Hosts.*
3. Shoghi Effendi, *Advent of Divine Justice,* ¶119.
4. Bahá'u'lláh, Súriy-i-Haykal, ¶174, in *Summons of the Lord of Hosts.*

5. Bahá'u'lláh, *Tablets,* p. 69.
6. Bahá'u'lláh, quoted in Shoghi Effendi, *Promised Day Is Come,* ¶287.
7. Bahá'u'lláh, *Gleanings,* no. 4.2.
8. Bahá'u'lláh, Súriy-i-Haykal, ¶118, in *Summons of the Lord of Hosts.*
9. Ibid., ¶105, 118.
10. Shoghi Effendi, *God Passes By,* p. 67.
11. Bahá'u'lláh, quoted in ibid., p. 109
12. Bahá'u'lláh, Súriy-i-Haykal, ¶103, 105, in *Summons of the Lord of Hosts.*
13. Bahá'u'lláh, *Gleanings,* no. 45.
14. Bahá'u'lláh, Súriy-i-Haykal, ¶102, in *Summons of the Lord of Hosts.*
15. Shoghi Effendi, *Promised Day Is Come,* ¶38.
16. Bahá'u'lláh, Súriy-i-Haykal, ¶179, in *Summons of the Lord of Hosts.*
17. Ibid., ¶126.
18. Ibid., ¶120.
19. Habakkuk 2:14
20. Bahá'u'lláh, Súriy-i-Haykal, ¶113, in *Summons of the Lord of Hosts.*
21. Bahá'u'lláh, *Proclamation,* p. 92.
22. Ibid., p. 93.
23. Ibid.
24. Bahá'u'lláh, Lawḥ-i-Aqdas, in *Tablets,* p. 13.
25. Bahá'u'lláh, *Proclamation,* p. 92.
26. Bahá'u'lláh, Súriy-i-Haykal, ¶127, in *Summons of the Lord of Hosts.*
27. Ibid., ¶106.
28. Matthew 24:29.
29. See Bahá'u'lláh, Kitáb-i-Íqán, ¶31–42.
30. Bahá'u'lláh, Lawḥ-i-Aqdas, in *Tablets,* p. 14.
31. *Chicago Daily News,* August 26, 1954.
32. John 3:10.
33. Bahá'u'lláh, *Proclamation,* p. 76.
34. Ibid., p. 75.
35. Ibid., pp. 75–76.
36. Bahá'u'lláh, Súriy-i-Haykal, ¶225, in *Summons of the Lord of Hosts.*
37. Matthew 15:14.
38. Bahá'u'lláh, *Proclamation,* p. 79.
39. Ibid., p 76.
40. Bahá'u'lláh, *Proclamation,* p. 78.
41. Bahá'u'lláh, Súriy-i-Haykal, ¶128, in *Summons of the Lord of Hosts.*
42. Bahá'u'lláh, Lawḥ-i-Aqdas, in *Tablets,* p. 14.

Chapter 15

1. Shoghi Effendi, *World Order of Bahá'u'lláh,* p. 42.
2. Bahá'u'lláh, Bishárát, in *Tablets,* p. 23.

3. Shoghi Effendi, *World Order of Bahá'u'lláh*, p. 65.

4. 'Abdu'l-Bahá, *Selections*, no. 2.7.

5. 'Abdu'l-Bahá, in *Bahá'í World Faith*, p. 400.

6. Shoghi Effendi, *Advent of Divine Justice*, ¶19.

7. Shoghi Effendi, *God Passes By*, p. 38.

8. Renan, *Les Apôtres*, quoted in Shoghi Effendi, *God Passes By*, p. 80.

9. Lord Curzon, quoted in ibid.

10. Shoghi Effendi, *God Passes By*, p. 81.

11. Ibid., p. 199.

12. Shoghi Effendi, *Messages*, pp. 37–38.

13. Bahá'u'lláh, *Gleanings*, p. 316.

Appendix

The epigraph for this chapter is from Bahá'u'lláh, Ishráqát, in *Tablets*, p. 118.

1. Bahá'u'lláh, Súriy-i-Mulúk, ¶12, in *Summons of the Lord of Hosts*.

2. Bahá'u'lláh, quoted in Shoghi Effendi, *God Passes By*, p. 230.

3. Shoghi Effendi, *World Order of Bahá'u'lláh*, p. 36.

4. For a detailed and well-written account of the story of Queen Marie's conversion to and public acknowledgment of her faith in Bahá'u'lláh, please see Della L. Marcus, *Her Eternal Crown*.

5. Bahá'u'lláh, *Gleanings*, no. 105.7.

6. Shoghi Effendi, *Promised Day Is Come*, p. 13.

7. Shoghi Effendi, *God Passes By*, pp. 389–95

8. Súrih of the Kings, a Tablet revealed by Bahá'u'lláh in Adrianople that deals with the responsibility of kingship. An English translation is available in *The Summons of the Lord of Hosts*.

9. See chapter 3, note 3.

10. Bahá'u'lláh, quoted in Shoghi Effendi, *God Passes By*, p. 253.

11. Translation from Samoan: "Loving greetings from all of us here in Samoa."

Bibliography

Works of Bahá'u'lláh

Epistle to the Son of the Wolf. 1st pocket-size ed. Translated by Shoghi Effendi. Wilmette, IL: Bahá'í Publishing Trust, 1988.

Gleanings from the Writings of Bahá'u'lláh. Translated by Shoghi Effendi. Wilmette, IL: Bahá'í Publishing, 2005.

The Hidden Words. Translated by Shoghi Effendi. Wilmette, IL: Bahá'í Publishing, 2002.

The Kitáb-i-Aqdas: The Most Holy Book. 1st pocket-size ed. Wilmette, IL: Bahá'í Publishing Trust, 1993.

The Proclamation of Bahá'u'lláh to the Kings and Leaders of the World. Haifa: Bahá'í World Center, 1967.

The Summons of the Lord of Hosts: Tablets of Bahá'u'lláh. Wilmette, IL: Bahá'í Publishing, 2006.

Tablets of Bahá'u'lláh revealed after the Kitáb-i-Aqdas. Compiled by the Research Department of the Universal House of Justice. Translated by Habib Taherzadeh et al. Wilmette, IL: 1988.

Works of 'Abdu'l-Bahá

A Traveller's Narrative Written to Illustrate the Episode of the Báb. Translated by E. G. Browne. New edition. Wilmette, IL: Bahá'í Publishing Trust, 1980.

The Promulgation of Universal Peace: Talks Delivered by 'Abdu'l-Bahá during His Visit to the United States and Canada in 1912. Compiled by Howard MacNutt. 2nd ed. Wilmette, IL: Bahá'í Publishing Trust, 1982.

Selections from the Writings of 'Abdu'l-Bahá. Compiled by the Research Department of the Universal House of Justice. Translated by a Committee at the Bahá'í World Center and Marzieh Gail. 1st pocket-size ed. Wilmette, IL: Bahá'í Publishing Trust, 1996.

Some Answered Questions. Compiled and translated by Laura Clifford Barney. 1st pocket-size ed. Wilmette, IL: Bahá'í Publishing Trust, 1984.

Works of Shoghi Effendi

The Advent of Divine Justice. 1st pocket-size ed. Wilmette, IL: Bahá'í Publishing Trust, 1990.

God Passes By. New ed. Wilmette, IL: Bahá'í Publishing Trust, 1974.

Messages to the Bahá'í World 1950–1957. Wilmette, IL: Bahá'í Publishing Trust, 1971.

The Promised Day Is Come. 1st pocket-sized ed. Wilmette, IL: Bahá'í Publishing Trust, 1996.

The World Order of Bahá'u'lláh: Selected Letters. 1st pocket-size ed. Wilmette, IL: Bahá'í Publishing Trust, 1991.

Compilations of Bahá'í Writings

Bahá'u'lláh, the Báb, and 'Abdu'l-Bahá. *Bahá'í Prayers: A Selection of Prayers Revealed by Bahá'u'lláh, the Báb, and 'Abdu'l-Bahá.* New ed. Wilmette, IL: Bahá'í Publishing Trust, 1991.

Bahá'u'lláh and 'Abdu'l-Bahá. *Bahá'í World Faith: Selected Writings of Bahá'u'lláh and 'Abdu'l-Bahá.* 2nd ed. Wilmette, IL: Bahá'í Publishing Trust, 1976.

Other Works

The Bahá'í World: An International Record, vol. 15, 1968–1973. Prepared under the supervision of the Universal House of Justice. Haifa: Universal House of Justice, 1975.

Balyuzi, H. M. *Edward Granville Browne and the Bahá'í Faith.* Oxford: George Ronald, 1970.

Blomfield, Lady [Sara Louisa]. *The Chosen Highway.* London: Bahá'í Publishing Trust, 1940.

Esslemont, J. E. *Bahá'u'lláh and the New Era: An Introduction to the Bahá'í Faith.* Wilmette, IL: Bahá'í Publishing, 2006.

Hazen, C. D. *Europe Since 1815.* New York: Henry Holt and Co., 1910.

Marcus, Della L. *Her Eternal Crown: Queen Marie of Romania and the Bahá'í Faith.* Oxford: George Ronald, 2000.

Nabíl-i-A'zam [Muḥammad-i-Zarandí]. *The Dawn-Breakers: Nabíl's Narrative of the Days of the Bahá'í Revelation.* Translated and edited by Shoghi Effendi. Wilmette, IL: Bahá'í Publishing Trust, 1932.

Sears, William. *Release the Sun.* Wilmette, IL: Bahá'í Publishing, 2003.

———. *Thief in the Night.* Oxford: George Ronald, 1961.

Taylor, A. J. P. *The Hapsburg Monarchy, 1809–1918: A History of the Austrian Empire and Austria-Hungary.* Chicago: University of Chicago Press, 1941.

INDEX

A

Abbás (witness against Bábís), 24–25

'Abdu'l-'Azíz, Sulṭán (ruler of the Ottoman Empire)
assassination of, 5–6, 149, 171
Bahá'u'lláh's messages to, 119–20, 127, 128, 141–42, 144, 148
banishes Bahá'u'lláh to Adrianople, 118
banishes Bahá'u'lláh to 'Akká, 125, 145
banishes Bahá'u'lláh to Constantinople, 115, 121
downfall of, 146

'Abdu'l-Bahá (Servant of Bahá'u'lláh; son of Bahá'u'lláh)
in 'Akká, 130, 159–62, 208
as architect of Bahá'í institutions, 158
on Bahá'u'lláh's arrival in Holy Land, 130
as Center of the Covenant, 157
on downfall of 'Abdu'l-Ḥamíd II, 163
dream of, 159–61
safety of, assured by British, 164–65
as Servant of Bahá'u'lláh, 157
service to sick and poor, 159

Tablets of the Divine Plan, 163
visit to Bahá'u'lláh in Black Pit, 26
world travels of, 157, 162, 165, 190

Abdu'l- Ḥamíd II (ruler of Ottoman Empire), 50, 149–50, 161, 171

Abraham, 127, 128

Abú-Tálib, Mírzá (Persian officer), 96–97

Acco. See 'Akká

Adrianople
Bahá'u'lláh banished to, 117–22
Bahá'u'lláh's prophecies about, 148
Bahá'u'lláh's writings while in, 122–24

Ahmad Sháh, 110

'Akká
Bahá'u'lláh in, 33–34, 49–50, 125–32, 155, 157–58, 174
decree banishing Bahá'u'lláh to, 125, 136–37
as "door of hope," 54, 75, 130, 174
foulness of, 130–31
Bahá'u'lláh's writings while in, 31–32, 99

Albanian monarchy, 171

Alexander II (czar of Russia)
assassination of, 6–7, 69
Bahá'u'lláh's letter to, 64–67, 71

For more information about the Baháʼí Faith,
or to contact the Baháʼís near you, visit
http://www.bahai.us/
or call
1-800-22-UNITE

Bahá'í
PUBLISHING
and the Bahá'í Faith

Bahá'í Publishing produces books based on the teachings of the Bahá'í Faith. Founded nearly 160 years ago, the Bahá'í Faith has spread to some 235 nations and territories and is now accepted by more than five million people. The word "Bahá'í" means "follower of Bahá'u'lláh." Bahá'u'lláh, the founder of the Bahá'í Faith, asserted that he is the Messenger of God for all of humanity in this day. The cornerstone of his teachings is the establishment of the spiritual unity of humankind, which will be achieved by personal transformation and the application of clearly identified spiritual principles. Bahá'ís also believe that there is but one religion and that all the Messengers of God—among them Abraham, Zoroaster, Moses, Krishna, Buddha, Jesus, and Muhammad—have progressively revealed its nature. Together, the world's great religions are expressions of a single, unfolding divine plan. Human beings, not God's Messengers, are the source of religious divisions, prejudices, and hatreds.

The Bahá'í Faith is not a sect or denomination of another religion, nor is it a cult or a social movement. Rather, it is a globally recognized independent world religion founded on new books of scripture revealed by Bahá'u'lláh.

Bahá'í Publishing is an imprint of the National Spiritual Assembly of the Bahá'ís of the United States.

Other Books Available
from Bahá'í Publishing

BAHÁ'U'LLÁH AND THE NEW ERA
An Introduction to the Bahá'í Faith
J. E. Esslemont
Trade Paper
$14.00 U.S. / $17.00 CAN
1-931847-27-4
978-1-931847-33-9

Bahá'u'lláh and the New Era shines as the most widely known and enduring textbook of the Bahá'í Faith. In this compact work, Esslemont comprehensively yet succinctly sets forth the teachings of Bahá'u'lláh, the Prophet and Founder of the Bahá'í Faith. He outlines the religion's early history, explains its theology, incorporates extracts from Bahá'í scripture, and provides information on Bahá'í spiritual practices. This is an excellent introduction to the Bahá'í Faith and the worldwide Bahá'í community, whose members represent what may well be the most ethnically and culturally diverse association of people in the world. The book, translated into some sixty languages since its initial publication in 1923, is a must-read for those interested in the study of the world's great religions.

FAITH, PHYSICS, AND PSYCHOLOGY
Rethinking Society and the Human Spirit
John Fitzgerald Medina
$17.00 U.S. / $20.00 CAN
Trade Paper
1-931847-30-4
978-1-931847-30-8

In *Faith, Physics, and Psychology,* John Medina explores new developments in three different but complementary movements— physics, psychology, and religion—that reflect a new understanding of what it means to be human. Written in the style of Fritjof Capra's *The Turning Point: Science, Society, and the Rising Culture,* with one critical difference: Medina includes discussions regarding the role of religion and spirituality in building a new society. Despite the progress of Western civilization in economic, scientific, and other areas, a lack of corresponding progress with respect to spiritual life has left much of society feeling disoriented and unbalanced. Medina's insight sheds light on ways to address this imbalance. The ultimate goal of this examination is to present a path toward a prosperous global civilization that fulfills humanity's physical, psychological, and spiritual needs.

GEMS FROM THE WORLD'S GREAT SCRIPTURES
Compiled and introduced by David Jurney
$12.00 U.S. / $15.00 CAN
Trade Paper
1-931847-43-6
978-1-931847-43-8

Powerful selections from the scriptures of six world religions that offer hope and solace to humanity.

Have you ever wondered what other religions teach about creation, prayer, and faith? *Gems from the World's Great Scriptures* answers these questions and more in an expertly arranged selection from the sacred scriptures of six religions: Buddhism, Christianity, Hinduism, Islam, Judaism, and the Bahá'í Faith. Each chapter covers a different topic and offers insight and inspiration on a theme assembled from the sacred writings of different faiths.

ONE WORLD, ONE PEOPLE
How Globalization Is Shaping Our Future
Gregory C. Dahl
$15.00 U.S. / $18.00 CAN
1-931847-35-5
978-1-931847-35-3

A thought-provoking examination of history, political influences, and the implications of global trends that reveals a brighter future for all of humankind.

Globalization and its impact on mankind are front and center in today's world! The media reports that planet Earth is rapidly becoming smaller and more interconnected. Many government policies, ideas, and institutions of the past are weakening in the face of the new challenges of globalization. Author Gregory C. Dahl, with twenty-seven years as an economist and senior official of the International Monetary Fund (IMF), offers a penetrating look at issues surrounding globalization and provides refreshing solutions to the many complex questions it raises. In *One World, One People* Dahl relies on his global experience with the IMF and insights provided by the Bahá'í Faith to suggest a promising future for all of humankind.

PARIS TALKS
Addresses Given by 'Abdu'l-Bahá in 1911
'Abdu'l-Bahá
$12.00 U.S. / $15.00 CAN
Trade Paper
1-931847-32-0
978-1-931847-32-2

This collection of inspiring and uplifting talks documents an extraordinary series of public addresses 'Abdu'l-Bahá gave on his historic trip to the West in the early twentieth century. Despite advanced age and poor health, he set out from Palestine in 1911 on a momentous journey to Europe and North America to share the teachings and vision of the Bahá'í

Faith with the people of the West. Addressing such subjects as the nature of humankind, the soul, the Prophets of God, the establishment of world peace, the abolition of all forms of prejudice, the equality of women and men, the harmony of science and religion, the causes of war, and many other subjects, 'Abdu'l-Bahá spoke in a profound yet simple manner that transcended social and cultural barriers. His deep spiritual wisdom remains as timely and soul-stirring as it was nearly a century ago. 'Abdu'l-Bahá, meaning *Servant of the Glory*, is the title assumed by 'Abbás Effendi (1844–1921)—the eldest son and appointed successor of Bahá'u'lláh, the Prophet and Founder of the Bahá'í Faith. A prisoner since the age of nine, 'Abdu'l-Bahá shared a lifetime of imprisonment and exile with his father at the hands of the Ottoman Empire. He spent his entire life in tireless service to, and promotion of, Bahá'u'lláh's cause and is considered by Bahá'ís to be the perfect exemplar of the Faith's teachings.

PARTNERS IN SPIRIT
What Couples Say about Marriages that Work
Heather Cardin
$12.00 U.S. / $15.00 CAN
Trade Paper
1-931847-31-2
978-1-931847-31-5

Partners in Spirit examines how a marriage can flourish in present-day society when the institution of marriage is seen by many as outdated and unnecessary. Heather Cardin incorporates interviews with over twenty married couples who share what has worked to strengthen their union during their years together. Their stories, hints, and advice illustrate the Bahá'í perspective of marriage, which involves an equal partnership in the spiritual development of both husband and wife. This provides a strong foundation for a happy and prosperous family life. The couples' advice on how to create these spiritual foundations can help both prospective marriage partners as well as those who have been married for years.

PEACE: MORE THAN AN END TO WAR
Foreword by Peter Khan
$18.00 U.S. / $21.00 CAN
Trade Paper
1-931847-39-8
978-1-931847-39-1

The horrors of innumerable conflicts currently blazing throughout the globe would seem to indicate that world peace is nothing more than a childish fantasy. But members of the Bahá'í Faith believe that the future is filled with hope and promise, for the Bahá'í writings state unequivocally that world peace is not only possible, it's inevitable.

How can this be? The selections from the Bahá'í writings in this compilation spell out how world peace can be achieved. They explain that humanity is in a transition from adolescence to adulthood, that the spiritual roots of peace must be identified, and that the barriers to peace—racism, extremes of wealth and poverty, the denial of the equality of men and women, and unbridled nationalism and religious strife—must be eliminated in order to lay the groundwork for true and lasting peace. The book discusses the essential Bahá'í principles of the oneness of humanity and the oneness of religion as being critical to the creation of a true and lasting peace.

Peace: More than an End to War is a blueprint both for the peace of the individual and the peace of our global society. This timely compilation can bring comfort to the world-weary souls who pause to explore the wisdom in its pages.

SEEKING THE WISDOM OF THE HEART
Reflections on Seven Stages of Spiritual Development
Patricia Romano McGraw, Ph.D.
$13.00 U.S. / $16.00 CAN
Trade Paper
1-931847-42-8
978-1-931847-42-1

Looking for the keys to true happiness and fulfillment? Join author and therapist Dr. Patricia Romano McGraw on a journey toward a deeper, more intimate knowledge of your spiritual self.

Through reflections, questions, and personal stories, McGraw leads readers on a journey toward enlightenment by narrating her own search for spiritual meaning as she reads, reflects, and writes in her personal journal about the Seven Valleys, an important work about spiritual development written by Bahá'u'lláh, the founder of the Bahá'í Faith. In her previous book, *It's Not Your Fault: How Healing Relationships Change Your Brain & Can Help You Overcome a Painful Past*, she offered a unique perspective on the effects of emotional trauma and explained how relationships can assist and accelerate the healing process. But how does one heal when there is no one around to help? Does healing necessarily require a relationship with a therapist? How does one take personal responsibility for his or her own inner healing? *Seeking the Wisdom of the Heart* discusses these questions and more, guiding the reader to begin living from the "inside out." Sharing experiences and reflections on her own "inside out" journey, Dr. McGraw offers hope for anyone who wants to begin the healing journey of spiritual growth.

THE SUMMONS OF THE LORD OF HOSTS
Tablets of Bahá'u'lláh
Bahá'u'lláh
$14.00 U.S. / $17.00 CAN
Trade Paper
1-931847-33-9
978-1-931847-33-9

The Summons of the Lord of Hosts brings together in one volume several major letters written by Bahá'u'lláh, prophet and founder of the Bahá'í Faith. In these magnificent documents he invites the monarchs and leaders of his time to accept the basic tenets of his Faith, sets forth the nature of his mission, and establishes the standard of justice that must govern the rule of those entrusted with civil authority. Written between 1868 and 1870, the letters call upon leaders of the East and West to accept Bahá'u'lláh's teachings on the oneness of God, the unity of all religions, and the oneness of humanity. Among the leaders specifically addressed are Napoleon III, Czar Alexander II, Queen Victoria, Náṣiri'd-Dín Sháh, and Pope Pius IX. A vitally important resource for those interested in the scripture and history of the world's great religions.

To view our complete catalog, please visit
http://books.bahai.us